David Bennett's p
end, and I feel sur
sexuality to God i
needs to consider.

Centre for Christian Apologetics

This is an incredibly raw and authentic book! David paints a beautiful and compelling picture of what it looks like to desire Christ above all else. His affections for Jesus make me excited to be a Christian.

—***Preston Sprinkle***, president, Center for Faith, Sexuality, and Gender

A refreshing and powerful book. This is one of the top books I will recommend to Christians who want to know how to better love their LGBTQI friends and also to seekers—whether gay or not—who are open to considering Jesus' invitation.

—***Sean McDowell***, professor, Biola University; speaker; author, *Same-Sex Marriage*

A timely, thoughtful, and often moving story which will be hugely helpful to a lot of people. David's honesty and humanity shine through these pages, even as he handles difficult questions through the lens of his experience. This is a gift to the contemporary church.

—***Andrew Wilson***, teaching pastor, King's Church London

Here is a voice as countercultural as it is compelling, capable of engaging the whole Christian community, whether gay or straight, in a vital debate. I have no doubt that David Bennett's story is going to become an essential part in a complex jigsaw for many.

—***Pete Greig***, 24-7 Prayer International and Emmaus Rd, Guildford

Many lesbian, gay, and bisexual people feel they cannot be true to both their sexuality and the Christian faith. David demonstrates that integrity and authenticity are possible for gay Christians, sharing beautiful insights about love, friendship, and following Jesus too.

—***Rev. Dr. Sean Doherty***, Christian ethicist; author, *The Only Way Is Ethics*

This book is designed to make all of us think about our ultimate love and to work through how we should engage in a long debated area, whether inside of the church or outside of it. It is well worth the read.

—***Darrell L. Bock,*** Senior Research Professor of New Testament Studies, Dallas Theological Seminary

David Bennett's book presents a particular lived Christian experience which deserves hearing. I am grateful to all who are contributing their learning, experience, study, and prayer to help us all to proclaim afresh the gospel of Jesus Christ.

—***Sentamu Eboracensis,*** Archbishop of York

One of the most significant books on one of the church's most pressing subjects by one of today's most inspiring young thought leaders. David Bennett is a prophetic witness, a truth teller, a tender pastor, and a faithful follower of Jesus. This generation needs to hear this man.

—***Rev. Simon Ponsonby,*** author; pastor of theology, St. Aldates Church, Oxford

This is the searingly honest story of one romanced by God against all expectations. Bennett's example of giving his whole self, including his sexual self, to the Christ who died for him is an act of Christian witness for our time.

—***Rev. Dr. Michael P. Jensen,*** rector, St. Mark's Darling Point, Sydney; author, *Martyrdom and Identity*

Riveting, extraordinary—quite extraordinary! I really think I could give this book to any contact I have and they'll be fascinated. I do wonder whether it will become a Christian classic of our time.

—***Rico Tice,*** All Souls Church London; author, *Christianity Explored*

I am particularly pleased to commend this book. It is an important contribution to the conversation. In a day when so often emotional story trumps thinking, David Bennett matches careful theological thinking with a truly compelling story.

—***Charlie Cleverly,*** rector, St. Aldates Oxford; member, General Synod of the Church of England

A WAR OF LOVES

THE UNEXPECTED STORY OF A GAY ACTIVIST DISCOVERING JESUS

DAVID BENNETT

ZONDERVAN®

ZONDERVAN

A War of Loves

This title is also available as a Zondervan ebook.

This title is also available as a Zondervan audiobook.

Requests for information should be addressed to:
Zondervan, *3900 Sparks Dr. SE, Grand Rapids, Michigan 49546*

ISBN 978-0-310-53810-3

Published in association with the literary agency of Mark Sweeney & Associates, Naples, Florida 34113.

Cover design: Micah Kandros Design
Cover art: Shutterstock
Interior design: Kait Lamphere

Printed in the United States of America

HB 09.30.2019

To my Lord and Savior, Jesus Christ, whose love radically transformed my life in that pub almost a decade ago

And to my father, Paul, who, after a stroke that almost took his life this last year, received Jesus Christ as his Lord and Savior

And to my mother, Anne-Marie, who believed in Jesus before I did, lovingly accompanied me in my search for truth, and whose steadfast love instilled in me the hope that carried me through the harder times

The only thing that counts is faith
expressing itself through love.

—The apostle Paul to the Galatians

CONTENTS

PART 3:
Wrestling with God: Sense and Sexuality

PART 4:
The New Identity

PART 5:
Reflections on Homosexuality and Christian Faithfulness

AUTHOR'S NOTE

Many of the stories I tell in this book are deeply personal, and so in most instances (except where permission has been given), to protect the privacy of those involved, I have altered names, places, and details while maintaining the storyline and events. The opinions in this book are my own and do not necessarily reflect those of the organizations, churches, people, or groups mentioned.

FOREWORD BY N. T. WRIGHT

This is a brave and wise book. The territory into which it leads us—in shockingly clear detail—is perhaps the most contested moral, social, and cultural issue of our times: the question of same-sex desire and practice. None of the issues is shirked here; no soft answers are on offer, no easy fudge to let us slide around the problems. David Bennett has lived for several years at the heart of the questions—or perhaps we should say that the questions have lived in his heart, like a wasps' nest buzzing angrily inside a room that ought to be a safe place. He has felt the pain of raging and unfulfilled desire, and also the pain of desire fulfilled but strangely unsatisfied. He has felt the anger of being patronized and dismissed by unthinking Christians, as well as the anger when, having discovered for himself the reality of Jesus as a living, loving, and challenging presence, he has often then been patronized and dismissed by the very people whose cause he had earlier, and loudly, advocated.

If all this sounds as though David Bennett will come across

as an angry young man, nothing could be farther from the truth. David looks back not *in* anger but *on* anger—and sees it, names it, and deals with it. He understands and sympathizes with those who see no problem in acting upon their same-sex desires or the way of life they shape around them; he disagrees with them but is able to explain why. He understands and has learned to forgive those whose practice of Christian faith has made them simply point a finger labelled "sin" at anyone who doesn't fit their stereotypes. The real heroes of his story, though, are quite different Christians who, with no loss of integrity or biblical wisdom, continued to love him and pray for him through some dark and stormy times.

David's account of his meeting with Jesus, and the transformation that this produced in his life, his mind, his body, his imagination, and his hopes, is alone worth double the price of the book. His conversion story, like all true conversion stories, is more complex and interesting than such a phrase might suggest. I was struck, in particular, by the way that before his meeting with Jesus, David positively *hated* the Bible. Since I have spent most of my life in love with the Bible and hoping to instill this love in others, it was and is good for me to be confronted with the sharp reminder that "that's how your stuff makes some people feel." But for those of us who engage in areas of Christian work other than frontline evangelism, his whole story is a wonderful encouragement: not that we ever supposed the gospel could no longer change lives, but that it's always good to hear fresh stories, vividly told, of how that change can happen despite the most unpromising starts.

There are, inevitably, places where we will agree to differ. David uses the language of LGBT and a few other initials as well; having lived in the world where those on the margins found a peer group with whom they could share sorrows and fears, he does not wish to turn his back on folk for whom that self-description is something of a lifeline. I have come to regard the list of initials LGBTQI as problematic, since each refers to quite different phenomena, sets of circumstances, assumptions, and challenges, and to lump them all together can, from the outside, look like a way of saying, "We're just going to live by whatever impulses we feel whenever we feel them." I stress *from the outside:* I greatly respect David's insider viewpoint and will, I hope, continue to learn from him.

Above all, I respect and salute David's resolute affirmation of *chastity:* of sexual fidelity in heterosexual marriage and sexual abstinence outside it. C. S. Lewis once remarked that when Charles Williams was lecturing in Oxford, the undergraduates were shocked because, having long supposed that the old rules about chastity were outdated, they were confronted with an author, literary critic, and lecturer who knew his texts like the back of his hand and was able to bring them gloriously to life, *and who passionately believed in chastity.* Hitherto they had supposed that anyone advocating sexual abstinence must have something wrong with them; now, suddenly, they discovered that the boot might be on the other foot. David Bennett's compassionate intelligence, his forthright tell-it-like-it-is memoir, and his rich theological understanding mean that when he advocates chastity, as he does in this book, nobody will be able to dismiss him in the way they might dismiss elderly theologians like the present writer.

Of course, if people prefer to work out their morality having checked in their brains at the door—a charge that applies equally to the unthinking Christian and to the unthinking secularist—then David Bennett's book will be a wake-up call. This is about *thinking through* what sexuality is really all about and what a wise and mature Christian reading of the Bible has got to do with it. If we can put thinking itself back on the agenda for these discussions, and then use that thinking to address in fresh ways the many-sided questions that force themselves upon us, we just might get somewhere. David Bennett's book will help at every stage of that urgently necessary process.

ACKNOWLEDGMENTS

I am profoundly grateful for the support of the Oxford Centre for Christian Apologetics (OCCA). The centre has become both my family and my professional community. Especially among them are Nancy Gifford, Amy and Frog Orr-Ewing, Mo Anderson, Michael Ramsden, Sanj and Kay Kalra, Sarah Davis, Karen and Joe Coffey, and Michael Suderman. Other friends I'd like to thank are my professor N. T. Wright, Dominic Steele, Hazel Thompson, Merrie Goddard, Anna Yearwood, Lauren Bolton, Ron Belgau, Simon Wenham, Coggin Galbreath, and Peter Hartwig, all of whom contributed to *A War of Loves* in different and important ways. I also credit so much to my aunt Helen, who helped me navigate church and so richly discipled me through this journey of faith. Finally, I would like to thank Wesley Hill, whose story was so pivotal to my story. I thank God for the vast multitude of often-hidden gay or same-sex-attracted Christians who faithfully follow Christ in this current climate. You are all an inspiration to me, and I hope this book will not just encourage you but also help to change the prejudices and pressures with which you bravely live.

PREFACE

As a nineteen-year-old atheist gay activist who felt rejected by Christianity, I had very little reason to believe in God. Then I encountered Jesus in a pub in the gay quarter of Sydney, Australia, and my life changed forever.

I wrote this book partly to help others navigate the tricky terrain of homosexuality and the Christian faith. However, my main reason for writing was simply to share how God's love has impacted my life. Rather than attempt to answer every question about homosexuality, I hoped to provide in this book's pages a clear picture of how I was reconciled to God. The gay and Christian communities are often seen as polar opposites: one a progressive, inclusive community, the other a community of oppressive, archaic laws. Having stood on both sides, I know the reality is far more complex.

My late colleague Nabeel Qureshi, author of the *New York Times* bestseller *Seeking Allah, Finding Jesus*, inspired me to write. Nabeel was diagnosed with stomach cancer when I began this book, and passed away in mid-2017. One evening in Oxford, just down the road from the famous Eagle and Child pub, Nabeel turned to me and said, "David, you will bless more people through a book than you ever will through speaking. It's time to write your story." Soon after, I met a prominent Christian evangelist, who agreed. "David," he told me, "you are called for a time such as this." I am grateful to them both for encouraging me forward.

A War of Loves is the story of how I met Jesus Christ, directly opposing the lie that God does not love gay or same-sex-attracted people, or any of us for that matter. I do three things in these pages.

1. Describe my personal quest for truth as someone from the gay community who became a Christian.
2. Provide insight into two worlds that often misunderstand each other.
3. Discuss the universal questions of love that both communities—indeed, all people—ask.

My prayer is that this book will be a resource not only on sexuality but also on how to know and experience God's love. None of us are below or beyond that love. I wish a book like this had existed when I first wrestled with the questions that prompted it. Within the book's limitations, I can't offer a systematic doctrinal solution to the questions that arise regarding same-sex desire. Yet I do attempt to point below the surface to share hard-fought truths I've discovered.

You have probably noticed that I call myself gay or same-sex attracted (SSA). By using these terms, I stand with the thousands of LGBTQI people around the world who suffer threats, hate crimes, imprisonment, internment or refugee camps, or even capital punishment. These terms are not an ultimate identity but a part of my personal reality preresurrection. I remember those who have deeply struggled or even committed suicide because they felt unable to reconcile their faith and sexuality. I stand too with my same-sex-attracted or gay Christian brothers and sisters who are living faithfully before Christ.

I call myself gay to remind broader groups that what I choose to do with my sexuality as a Christian is caught up in my worship of God, and that the fundamental human desire for intimacy is ultimately fulfilled in a relationship with Jesus and what he accomplished on the cross for us all.

I call myself celibate because I have chosen, by God's grace, to give my sexuality to Jesus Christ. The scriptural teaching on sex is reasonably clear, but there is so much more to the experience of being a gay or same-sex-attracted person than language-games, prohibitions, or information.

This book is not essentially about being gay. It is about finding a greater identity in Jesus Christ and becoming a son of God. My ultimate identity is found in Jesus Christ, but the reality of my same-sex desires is an important part of that story. Amid all the confusion around issues of faith and sexuality, I feel much like C. S. Lewis in *Shadowlands:* "I have no answers anymore . . . only the life I have lived."[1] In the following pages, I invite you to consider the message of the glorious gospel that has impacted my life through this, my story.

PART I

THE SEARCH

CHAPTER 1

COMING OUT

You, LORD, brought me up from the realm of the dead;
you spared me from going down to the pit.

—Psalm 30:3

It was the first Friday evening since moving to the Sydney harborside, and a day after my fourteenth birthday. From a high sandstone outcrop bordering the water, I watched the sun set over a small mooring of boats. The chiming of their sails rang out from the cove and over the peninsula. A blush of ochre tinted the sky. Sydney Harbour Bridge was hidden behind the eucalyptus trees, but the cityscape was in view on the horizon, iridescent with skyscrapers.

Such beauty made me ache for someone to share it with—another young man. Standing in my untucked school uniform, I peered over the ledge, where water lapped at oyster-laden rocks down below. The ferry glided on the incoming tide with its monotone growl. Tears welled up from what I knew was true. *I feel light enough to jump over the edge.* The crushing ocean seemed lighter than my unwanted desires, and my feet dared me to step over the edge of the cliff. I pulled back in sudden horror. My heart raced as I ran home and the dusk fell.

Not long after, I found myself at school. The recess bell rang throughout the school grounds, and the summer sun shone over the brick buildings. More than a thousand boys, each in the traditional uniform of red-lined navy blazers, white shirt, grey woolen trousers, black shoes, and a navy blue tie, poured through the grounds to the entrances of the Anglican chapel. It was a chaotic sight that somehow always managed to become orderly in minutes as everyone lined up to enter. We resembled an army regiment at attention, with just a few naughty soldiers out of formation.

Soon the sound of hundreds of adolescent boys singing awkwardly from hymnbooks filled the chapel. As I took my place among the pews, my vision blurred. I had fond memories of singing solos in the boys' choir before my voice broke, and of my favorite soprano solo: Howard Goodall's "The Lord Is My Shepherd." But today I was silent, repulsed by the thought of singing to a God I knew didn't exist, since his only response to my unspoken questions had been a deafening silence.

My hardworking agnostic parents had attained an upper middle class lifestyle. Life was good, but I was often unhappy and lonely, surrounded by the boredom and beauty of the suburbs. I dreamed about escaping to the city, which offered the liberty and sophistication I craved.

Our extended family had a wide range of religious beliefs and convictions. With my Christian relatives, I often heard strange terms used to describe homosexuality. Either it was a kind of spiritual oppression that needed to be prayed away, or it was a result of sexual abuse that required serious healing. None of these pseudotheories fit me.

For other Christians, homosexuality was the worst of sins

and homosexuals were God's enemies. This rhetoric missed the reality of what I was going through and closed me down to the honest confession and self-acceptance I deeply desired ever since I awoke at the onset of puberty to my attraction to men. The widely variant views of why people are homosexual—genetics? abuse? father issues? something else entirely?—bombarded me. I felt so confused.

On top of this, coming to terms with my attractions at the age of fourteen meant entering an ugly, polarized culture war that spanned the globe. All I wanted was a place where I could be honest. All I wanted was to find a boyfriend and escape the monotony, and ignorance I perceived in the people around me. Then I could finally be accepted and move on with my life.

One night I cried out, "Take these attractions away!" Nothing changed, and the silence drove me farther away from Christianity. The attractions I'd felt since age nine weren't about a lifestyle I'd chosen. They were about who I was.

Since a young age, I'd understood that a person's romantic attractions shape their humanity. Love makes us human, and without it, life is not worth living. I wanted all that life had to offer, so I knew I had to keep my distance from those Christians who were getting in my way. Still, the message that God didn't approve of people like me gnawed at my conscience.

For a year, I tried to think of the opposite sex the way my peers did. Then I dismissed such thoughts as ridiculous. I didn't believe in God, so why worry anymore? My growing interest in men's bodies had only increased, and the nervousness I experienced around certain members of the same sex brought me to a place where I knew I was attracted exclusively to men. I even wrote a poetry anthology about my inner secret.

As the chapel service ended, I concluded I could no longer put off the reality of my attractions. The more I denied them, the more miserable I became.

SEARCHING THROUGH SCIENCE

Why was I gay? Shows like *Queer as Folk* or *Will and Grace* simply told me I was made or born this way. That wasn't particularly specific.

I began searching for an answer. I read through nature versus nurture arguments in studies. I googled everything I could find.

Simon LeVay's research in 1991 showed there was a substantial difference between the brains of gay and straight men in the hypothalamus.[2] Other studies found that gay men responded to the pheromones of men, not women.[3] Studies on identical twins showed a genetic contribution to sexual orientation, but not a genetic determination.[4] More recent studies had shown the potential influence of the hormonal environment of the womb.[5] Sigmund Freud's psychoanalytic theory for homosexual behavior linked same-sex attraction to parental relationships. Environment? Biology? Genetics? Nurture? Hormones? Conditioning? Nothing was conclusive. Little was clear or known about the why of it. And that almost crushed me. Understanding myself seemed completely out of reach.

A war developed in me about how to understand this part of my identity. The belief that we're all born this way wasn't the whole story. I was more confused than ever.

READING THROUGH RELIGION

Since science couldn't tell me why I was gay, I decided to try religion—and didn't make it far.

Even if there was a Christian God, I felt disqualified from a relationship with him because of who I wanted to love. Yet I longed for intimacy of the spirit as much as that of the body—perhaps more.

Why did the relationship between Christianity and homosexuality have to be so complex? I read different Christian perspectives, progressive to traditional. Eventually I accepted the view that the apostle Paul was obviously unaware of any faithful, monogamous relationships between two members of the same sex. I decided his writing was a cultural artifact that didn't hold the authority orthodox Christians gave it.

Throughout my schooling, I had been exposed to Christianity through camps, youth groups, and church activities. I always felt unable to belong, especially when I heard their teachings on homosexuality. Being gay was explained as rooted in a bad relationship with my father or other masculine figures. Whenever I heard this explanation used to dismiss the gay community, my stomach twisted. I, like many others I spoke to online, had a great relationship with my father. I had never been abused. My Greek father was an ambitious software executive and a generous man. We were different from each other, but I always knew he loved me. Our relationship was quite good; the father-figure story didn't fit, and there were many gay people who had great relationships with their same-sex parent.

I felt like Christians were explaining me away, not entering into my experience. That was bad enough, but their explanation wasn't even any good! I found it frustratingly hypocritical that Christians, who worshiped a savior of transparency and truth, couldn't deal with my being honest about my humanity. Their obvious prejudice toward gay people only pushed me farther away. I perceived that perhaps homosexuality unearthed deeper problems in the church, especially an obsession with sexual desire.

All I knew was that I was gay, that I didn't choose it, and that the God represented by many Christians could not be an all-loving, all-powerful creator. How could he allow my fundamental human desire for romantic companionship to be directed toward the same sex and then reject me because of it? My unchosen desire was incompatible with the term righteous, so I was hopelessly stuck in the "sinful" category.

Without knowing exactly why I was gay, I found it hard to summon the courage to come out. I was in awe of others I read about online who had come out to their families, schools, or faith communities. I wanted to take this step for the other gay kids at my school whose lives might be significantly improved by my action. But how to start? At school, insecure boys used *gay* as a casual insult.

Most of my school friends were agnostics or atheists and were more in touch than the Christian kids. To us, Christianity seemed like a club with narrow, oppressive political values. We aspired to the real freedoms we knew existed beyond it. Privately, I was still captured by what I knew of Jesus and reasoned that he had been the greatest human being in history. But he'd been lost in a human-invented religion that tried to make him into a god. I pictured this human-invented religion like the pencil sketches in my Good News Bible, portraying a cookie-cutter Jesus who made me gay (that would explain it!), then cruelly condemned me for it.

Yet I had a persistent inkling that maybe there was a deeper answer in those pages.

THE GRACE OF A GIRLFRIEND

As I was struggling with all of this, I started seeing a girlfriend, Liz, from our sister school. She made me laugh and had a kindness and warmth that attracted me to her. She liked me because I was different—I danced better than most at our school dances, and I didn't stare at her midsection when we talked, like most of the other adolescent boys.

One afternoon we went to a film. *Planet of the Apes* was the only one showing. After I bought our tickets, we both burst out laughing when she said that all told, I won the award for the most unromantic boyfriend ever.

We enjoyed the hammy moments of the film and she held my hand for the first time, but I was preoccupied. By the time the credits rolled, I'd decided to tell her my secret. I knew she was a safe person, trustworthy and mature. I also knew my secret meant the end of our relationship, and I felt the weight of something like guilt in the pit of my stomach.

As we walked out of the cinema, she glanced at me. "I'm sorry this was such a bad third date!" I said.

She took my hand. "David, why does it seem like you never want to kiss me or be close?"

"That's a hard question. I'm not really sure why I'm like this," I said, looking away.

"Like what?" she asked gently.

"I've wanted to tell you for a long while," I said, swallowing.

"Remember my favorite park I showed you a few weeks ago? I've never had a suicidal thought in my life, but when I was there a while back, I wanted to jump off the cliff's edge, and just about did it. I was petrified.

"I have to tell you, Liz—I've been attracted to guys since I can remember. I need to finally face it. I didn't choose it, and it isn't going away."

As I spoke, relief came. And with it apprehension for what I had just voiced into the world.

Liz looked away, quiet. After a long silence, she bounced back with her usual direct but affectionate manner. "You need to come out, David. Need to. Tell your parents, okay? Promise?"

She hugged me, and I heard both sadness and concern in her voice. "It's important you be honest about who you are. You can't live with that eating away at you."

TELLING MY MOTHER

I came out to my group of close school friends later that week. It felt amazing to be myself, fully accepted by them. But they weren't my biggest hurdle. By that Saturday, I couldn't keep the truth from my mother any longer. (I usually told her everything.)

I didn't expect negativity. I knew Mum had many gay friends, and she had raised me to love and respect gay people. Her friends, Chris and Tim, a couple from her university days, were our good friends. They had taken me to see musicals when I was a toddler. I felt a deep affinity with them that I later understood was related to their being an openly gay couple, committed to each other for more than forty years, even when discrimination toward gay people was far worse. But I still felt unbelievably sensitive about broaching this with her. How would she respond when it was a son?

I thought about all this as we drove to a friend's birthday party. When we pulled up to the house, she smiled at me with her kind hazel eyes and kissed me goodbye.

I looked out the window of her blue Volvo, my hand hesitating on the door handle.

"Bye, David!"

There was a pause. "Mum, before I go, I have to tell you something."

"What, darling?" she said, her tone changing to concern when she saw my pained expression.

It had come to the moment, and it was too much. Why? I looked away. "I don't think I can actually say it."

"Have you got someone pregnant?"

I shook my head, fighting the urge to laugh. Would teenage fatherhood be preferable to this?

"Are you gay?" she said as the summer humidity began to fog the windows.

"Yes, Mum," I said. Those two words felt impossibly heavy.

She reached over, wrapped me in her arms, and wept. I'll never forget the feeling of the leather seats, her wet tears on my clothing. And in that moment, I felt peace—real peace—for the first time in years, for the first time since I'd discovered I was gay. And I somehow knew that her tears weren't about her at all; they were about me. She knew how much harder my life would be as a gay man. "I'm just sad that you'll have to live with the difficulties so many gay people do," my mother said. "But we love you no matter what, David. We are with you."

By the time I got home from the party, my mother had told my father. He was fully accepting too, even if his vision of my marrying and having a family had been shattered. He proudly told me he looked forward to one day meeting my partner.

Conversations continued in the following weeks about whether this was a stage. But I knew it wasn't. Mum took me to visit a psychiatrist who was an expert in sexual health. He kindly helped me accept myself. He told me my attractions were just like having a different hair or eye color and should be a source of pride.

Coming out was deeply difficult, but it was liberating. Finally, I could be completely real with my parents.

And for a little while, I felt a respite from the war within.

CHAPTER 2

QUEST FOR SPIRITUALITY

I am the Lord, and there is no other; apart from me there is no God. I will strengthen you, though you have not acknowledged me.

—*Isaiah 45:5*

Now that I was being honest with my parents about this significant part of who I was, I wanted to reexamine the rift between homosexuality and religion. Were they really incompatible? Or was there some truth beyond traditional Christianity, which, I was convinced, stood in the way of LGBTQI people's rights? I wondered, still unable to shake that sense of something *real* about Jesus.

I asked Mum to drive me to an affirming (of gay marriage) church on the other side of town.

We pulled up to the dull-red-brick building, adorned with rainbow flags and a big "Welcome" sign. As we entered late, we saw they were having a Communion service. The congregation was split between two groups of people—one of which, I would later learn, didn't believe in Jesus' physical resurrection.

The paradox of this church intrigued me, and I was amazed to see LGBTQI people together believing in Jesus. Yet it was the ideal of marriage, not faith, that attracted me to this church. I wanted desperately to be married. I pictured myself beside a creatively gifted, intellectually bright, and handsome husband. We'd live in an apartment in Paris, adopt an orphan, take in a poodle.

Gay marriage seemed an essential right. It harmed no one. I had no idea why the majority of Christians, who held moral sway in society, were obsessed with what others did in their bedrooms. But after attending this church for some time, something felt missing. Deep down, it seemed wrong that they were separated from the rest of the church. I also thought the arguments I read by Bishop John Shelby Spong, their favorite theologian, didn't make honest sense of the Scriptures or reconcile with traditional Christian beliefs, like the resurrection. Mum felt the same way. I didn't believe in it, sure, but I couldn't make sense of the incoherences either. We decided to leave.

Christianity continued to haunt me and my mother, though. In following months, as I came out to Christian members of my extended family, there were difficult conversations about faith and sexuality. "David, you can't accept Satan!" one of my cousins said. "*He* gave you these desires. You just need God to help you change." Well, that explained a lot—the devil made me do it, apparently.

That was it. I stopped trying to reconcile my homosexuality with Christianity and determined to find fulfillment through some other spiritual path.

LOOKING FOR SPIRITUALITY

As the years of high school passed, I caught the train to downtown Sydney often. I spent countless hours at Adyar, then the largest new age bookstore in the southern hemisphere. The store and its regulars were my oasis in a boring suburban existence of Saturday sports and my all-boys school.

I developed a crush on one of the front counter cashiers, whom I often observed behind the labyrinth of bookshelves. His dark curly hair and broad smile revealed a peace and security I'd never seen in another gay man. I found out he was a witch; he wore a pentagram, a five-pointed star used by the Wiccan religion, visibly under his shirt. "The four points represent the four elements—water, wind, fire, and earth—and the fifth is spirit," he explained.

He didn't fit the diabolical picture of witches I'd been given by Christians. He seemed a deeply spiritual person who accepted his sexuality and welcomed me with ease. I wanted that calm confidence he had.

I asked him for books on Wicca and tried to learn everything I could about "the craft." I was desperate to find a universal power or mystical reality, and Wicca allowed me to shape my own worship. I enjoyed the honesty and comradery of the neo-pagan community and even tried to start a half-hearted coven at my school.

Learning about the church's historical treatment of witches and people who practiced other spiritualties confirmed to me that Christianity was a grave, hypocritical evil, responsible for so much pain in the world. As I got to know others, it was clear many LGBTQI people became Wiccans directly because of how the church had treated them. Christianity was the enemy. Not only its people but the worldview it espoused.

But rejecting it also left an intellectual and philosophical void. For all its attraction, Wicca was impossible to test rationally, and I saw it was a too-easy projection of how I wanted the divine to be. I felt like I was bottoming out. *If the gods we worship are exactly like us,* I wondered, *are we just creating divinity to be like us or in our own image?* I decided it was no longer for me and saw no further hope in it than what I already had.

So on I went, and on, always further on. Truth seemed to slip farther away the more I grasped at it. Eventually I read up on Theravada Buddhism, becoming enthralled by the person and teaching of Siddhartha Buddha, and decided to become a Buddhist. Buddhism seemed like a peaceful belief system with a certain logic to it that could be compatible with the more demonstrable parts of my worldview, while happily ignoring the issue of sexuality.

For most of 2005, I followed the teachings of the Dalai Lama, who argued that the center of the human problem was desire itself. Through meditative practices and self-denial, we could reach nirvana, a state of perfect consciousness. I attempted to move through the different levels of attainment by ridding myself of desire, even the desire for romantic love.

But eventually I became disillusioned with Buddhism too. Its negative view of human desire and its notion of dharma condemned humanity to an eternal cycle of self-justification and reincarnation. Didn't our desires *matter?* Weren't they part of what made us human? And if so, didn't they point to something outside us, something we long for and were made to experience?

My quest for love must have a reason behind it, I thought.

AN OFFER OF GRACE

I'd become known around school for my opinions and desperately wanted to see a protective policy for LGBTQI students. Eric seemed to respect me for it. His reaction was different from those of the other Christian friends I had in my classes. He didn't annoy me as much as the other Christians, who, I was convinced, believed just because of their upbringing.

But still, no matter how I tried, I couldn't escape the influence of Christianity, at home or at school. It irked me. Whether in class or in casual conversations, it seemed like Jesus would not stay tidily out of my life.

My friend Eric caught up with me one day as we came out of choir practice. "David, do you know what grace is?"

The question was so out of the blue, I was taken aback. "I don't know if there's any of that for LGBTQI people from your ridiculous God," I replied.

"I just think it's important for you to know that God accepts you and GLBTQI people," he said.

"Eric, it's L-G-B-T-Q-I—lesbian, gay, bisexual, transgender, queer, intersex," I snapped.

He looked hurt, and sure, I had spoken harshly. But he asked for it, right? *Do I know what grace is? Who does he think he is?* But, apparently unable to take a hint, he continued walking with me on our way to our Christian studies class.

"I still don't understand why this school makes Christian classes mandatory," I grumbled, trying to change the subject.

"Jesus is the greatest figure in history. Don't you think we should learn about him?"

I tensed. My mother had surprised me recently, saying she was considering becoming a Christian—like, really believing, not just attending services. I responded to Eric with pent-up anger. "Hey, my mother's been talking about actually believing in your imaginary God. I just told her she needs to choose between the delusion in her head and her real son right in front of her."

He seemed excited by the prospect of my mum believing. "I don't need this from you too, man," I continued. "Come on. You really think she should pick an immaterial delusion over her flesh-and-bone son? She's even saying stuff like by loving God, maybe she'll love me better. I told her she has to choose. Him or me. I hope she picks the one who, you know, actually exists."

Entering the classroom, we picked up red imitation leather Bibles and sat down. I rolled my eyes at Eric. The reverend at our school had given us all diaries in which to write our thoughts, questions, and objections as part of our final mark for the class. I would often tap my shoe as the reverend spoke, largely unconvinced by his answers to student questions that cropped up as we read.

That day we started our reading in Luke 16. Jesus was telling a parable about the afterlife, and as we read, I felt ready to explode. Was I the only one seeing through this farce? It seemed so fake.

My hand shot up at question time. "Sir, I don't understand how you can believe in God or this book. We know so much about the universe and science, and we're still talking about fairy tales? Not just harmless ones either; church history is a history of oppression. It's delusional or worse to believe that without Jesus Christ someone's going to hell for things that aren't even their fault."

The reverend smiled kindly. "David, Jesus welcomes any questions we have. There's freedom in belief, not just a history of oppression."

"But why are we wasting our time reading a dead book?" I was getting closer to the real question, the one I'd been dancing around since my hand shot up. "And what about your view on gay marriage?"

Everyone stared, like I'd stepped over a line. Not that they were surprised, surely, with the question coming from me.

"I'm gay," I continued. "So what about people like me? Are we loved by God, as you claim, or are we unable to enter the kingdom of God, like Paul says in 1 Corinthians?"

That was one way to quiet down a room of high schoolers. But our teacher seemed unfazed. "Let's talk after class," he said. "You're asking an important question. It requires a much longer answer than I can give without delaying the class."

At the end of class, as students stood and chattered, filing out the door, the reverend caught me before I could leave. I was still fuming. He handed me a black notebook. "Write it all down," he said, "all your questions and objections. I promise to respond." I took it and nodded, thinking that the poor man had no idea what he'd just signed up for.

I wrote and wrote and wrote. I worked to organize my questions, from the most pressing and concrete to the more abstract, and every week he would respond to one. It was obvious that he was taking time, really engaging, with a kind of intellectual honesty that disturbed me. It was easier to dismiss believers as ignorant, cruel, or numb to real issues. But he didn't let me dismiss him. It was too evident that he cared.

It was the first time I'd felt loved by a Christian. He took each question seriously and wrote back with his opinion. We covered gay marriage and the Bible's stance on homosexuality. We covered the historical accuracy of events in Genesis; the trustworthiness of the Gospels; Paul's view of women; evolution; the problem of suffering; and the question of salvation and other religions.

But I remained unconvinced. Homosexuality was my stumbling block. He talked about God's love for gay people, but I still couldn't comprehend how, if I were to become a Christian, my homosexuality was reconcilable with Scripture. I just didn't see it.

Around this time, I was also close to fully embracing atheism. I'd met with my English teacher, also willing to give my unusual questions extra attention, and my interests started to turn to postmodernism. I was attracted by the agnosticism of existentialists like Jean-Paul Sartre, Albert Camus, and Simone de Beauvoir and had decided to take extra units in French to better understand their work.

It felt like my mind was being stretched between two points that were quickly moving apart. I would have to choose one or the other or snap clean in two. Christianity seemed impossible to embrace with intellectual or personal honesty. And yet the atheists brought with them a profound sense of emptiness. For all my anger at the church, for all my objections, for all the oppression, there was meaning there. Disagree, sure, but I could not fully dismiss it.

Christians? *Hypocrites, of course,* I thought. *All of them.* But were the secular atheists any better? Their problems ran just as deep, it seemed; they were just different. There was a hypocrisy about atheistic existentialism, a fundamental self-contradiction. Try as I might, I could not make it add up. If I took moral responsibility for my own actions, the consequences would outweigh my capacity to repair them. I would be condemned to always be like Sisyphus, rolling the boulder of my choices up and down the mountain of life. And was that it? Was that constant torment of consciousness what it really meant to be human? Was helplessness the result of rationality?

I'd abandoned what I thought was an absurd world of the

spirit, whether ensconced in high-church hymns or enshrouded in adolescent witches' covens. But would existentialism leave me just as empty?

De Beauvoir's heart had been crushed by Sartre. They had it all figured out but couldn't even live well with each other. There had to be something better, but I felt farther away from it than ever as the weeks went by.

I eventually resumed wrestling with that hated book I could not shake off. One night I opened the Bible and read all six passages dealing with homosexuality. By the end, I threw it down, determined to never read it again.

The Bible was a dangerous book. It taught, I thought, that simply by being who I was, I was the worst of sinners, unable to inherit the kingdom of God and unacceptable to the very one who made me. What kind of God makes a person with one hand and condemns him with the other? What kind of good news is that? No good news at all. I saw it with a terrible finality that, for the moment, ended all my questions.

The Christian faith was bad news. For everyone. It was especially terrible news for gay people. I had no love for this cruel, imaginary God and never would. To love him would be the ultimate betrayal of myself.

I decided that night, with my Bible open and a seething fury in my heart, that I was going to dedicate my life to stopping the Christian faith.

CHAPTER 3

THE FRENCH EXCHANGE

> The Lord appeared to us in the past, saying: "I have loved you with an everlasting love; I have drawn you with unfailing kindness."
>
> —*Jeremiah 31:3*

How adult I felt then! Wrestling with the foundational questions of existence has a way of growing you up. But really I was still a young teen.

When I was fifteen, I found myself at the end of a two-month student exchange in France. One evening, my host family and I had returned from a holiday in Ardèche, and as I unpacked in my room in their apartment, with its beautiful parquet floor and high roof, I looked out again at a tiny café where a regular always sat smoking a cigarette, reading the newspaper, and sipping his coffee. That winter, I had mimicked him by reading or writing letters by my window, coffee in hand. Often the sound of organ music serenaded me as my French dad practiced for Mass.

I found the godlessness of France attractive, and its staunch separation of church and state, called *laïcité,* comfortable. During my stay, I had attempted to read *Existentialism Is a Humanism* by

Jean-Paul Sartre, using my high school French skills. I finally deciphered Sartre's thesis: unlike Søren Kierkegaard or Fyodør Dostoevsky, he didn't believe God was necessary to be an existentialist. I too didn't need a belief in God for meaning and significance. I could happily invent that myself.

"Existentialism is not atheist in the sense that it would exhaust itself in demonstrations of the non-existence of God," Sartre wrote. "It declares, rather, that even if God existed that would make no difference . . . what man needs is to find himself again and to understand that nothing can save him from himself, not even a valid proof of the existence of God."[6]

France represented my freedom from all those fundamentalists with their talk of a judgmental God. As an agnostic atheist, I also now identified as an existentialist in Sartre's line.

Before long, I said my goodbyes to my host family. My French dad accompanied me to the *Lyon-Part Dieu* station and placed a CD in my hand on which he had stored a short film he had made with footage from my trip. On it was a quote from my favorite French film, *Amélie*. He hugged me and gave me two big *bisous* on my cheek.

All the Australian students staying in France met for a reunion in Paris before heading home. As we huddled at the train station and ordered espressos to go, we were abuzz with the delight of our experiences. Later that night, I felt a deep liberation as I sat in my parquet-floored hostel room.

But I was also sad. A secret internet love interest had sent his last letter weeks before, breaking off our relationship. As I explored Paris with my friends and found myself in the center of Paris's lively gay community in the Marais district, my heart ached to find love. Surveying the cafés, Jewish delis, and clubs concentrated in what seemed a cosmopolitan utopia, I wished I could stay there forever. Yet in this free, secular space, I sensed an open wound in my heart. My search for God had waned, and a painful desire for romantic love had replaced it.

IMPOSSIBLE SPIRES

As I waved goodbye to my friends in France, I boarded a plane for London to see some of the United Kingdom with my mother's ex-colleague, Daniel, before returning home to Australia. He was a kind man and an ardent atheist. We were fond of each other. He knew I had rejected the Christian faith after coming out a year before, and we shared a similar disdain for religion.

Daniel collected me from London's Heathrow Airport in his blue Ford. We were soon out in the English countryside, and I sat quietly, taking in the lush green landscape for the first time. Daniel had blond hair, thinning on top, and a charming gap in his teeth when he smiled. As we drove, thatched houses, sheep, tall birch trees, and flat pastures blooming with spring flowers dazzled me after the long French winter.

After settling in at Daniel's lovely Cotswolds cottage just outside Strafford-upon-Avon, we decided over tea to see Oxford the next day. We mapped out each site, with our final evening stop at Christ Church Meadow. My image of Oxford was rather grand. It was an idea to me, the place of an intellectual golden age, the enchanting domain of masters of the imagination like Lewis and Tolkien. It was the university of people who made history.

The next morning was blue and beautiful. Passing for an hour through verdant fields, we finally entered Oxfordshire.

After touring colleges and visiting the Ashmolean Museum, Daniel insisted we stop at the famous Blackwell's bookstore. He said he'd buy me a book of my choosing and select one for me as a gift. As we searched the enormous underground selection of books, he came back to me, smiling.

"I think this will really help you. Your mother has told me you've been on a spiritual quest to find some kind of faith," he said as he passed me *The Selfish Gene* by Richard Dawkins. "Also, with your interest in Sartre, Dawkins will help you with the freedom of realizing there is no God. We can all get on with our lives!"

I was charmed by the intensity of Daniel's tone. As we walked, he explained how evolution alone explained our search for love and transcendence. He reiterated how we had to rise above blind faith to regain a human ethic of generosity, even if we were born selfish animals bent on our own fear-based survival.

The conversation turned to my future as we passed into a huge meadow where college rugby teams were training. We paused, watching the players. My breath caught at this stunning vista of Christ Church and Corpus Christi colleges, with the setting sun reflecting off the millennium-old sandstone buildings. *I will never study here. I'll never be good enough,* I thought. I would remember these thoughts and words of self-doubt years later when I returned to Oxford.

My time in France and the UK brought me great freedom. But the future remained unclear, and my desire to find love was greater than ever. I wondered if I would ever find the belonging and intimacy that I longed for with every atom of my being.

CHAPTER 4

BOYFRIENDS AND PSYCHICS

Now, this is what the LORD says—he who created you, Jacob, he who formed you, Israel: "Do not fear, for I have redeemed you; I have summoned you by name; you are mine."

—*Isaiah 43:1*

Romantic relationships and sex were everywhere and in everything I talked about with my teenage friends. Frankly, I was exhausted by my sexuality being just a theory.

It was almost the school year, and I decided to have my three best friends over to celebrate. My parents had gone away for the evening, and I ordered pizza for a movie night and slumber party. We could enjoy our newfound teenage freedom and stay up as late as we liked.

My three friends were all so different. But one of them stood out. Really stood out. Andrew, who joined us from the more rebellious group of boys at school, was deeply perceptive and had a quick intelligence I found appealing. We were in the same

English class, and an emotional chemistry and friendly rivalry had grown between us as we discussed books, especially French writers and Shakespeare. We loved the same bands and planned to buy tickets to the same concerts. We had so much in common.

I sat next to Andrew on the old green leather couch and pulled up a big woolen blanket for us to ward off the early autumn chill. As we started the final film, I felt Andrew's hand slide next to me under the blanket. I was shocked. Nothing like this had happened before. My heart rate doubled—or at least it felt like it did.

The intensity of my fifteen-year-old reaction was hard to handle. All the pent-up excitement from years of watching gay sitcoms flooded through me. I reached my hand over to reciprocate. *Is Andrew gay?*

Andrew looked over and smiled, and my heart thudded as I processed his advance. I gestured to go upstairs to my bed, leaving the others to the film. He looked straight back at me. *This is it,* I thought. *This is the moment I've waited for.* My desires were about to be more than theoretical. I couldn't wait to get to my room.

But as we both lay heatedly back on the bed, Andrew suddenly pushed me away. "Oh, God, no! I'm not gay. I can't believe this has happened! What was I thinking?" Sitting up, he hit his hand against his forehead.

"Andrew, it's okay. There's nothing wrong with being gay," I said, trying to comfort him.

"Get away from me!"

"Let's at least chat this through . . . or we could just hold each other?" I said, realizing he was slipping away.

"You're the one who did this to me!" he said with a scowl.

"Andrew, you need to accept yourself. Don't take this out on me," I whispered, afraid of waking the others.

"I'm not gay, David. I'm not interested in you, and I don't find you in *any* way attractive. This whole thing is over," he said. He moved off the bed and hit his head hard against the wall. I tried to stop him, but he pulled away and slammed the door behind him.

My heart dropped. My first sexual encounter was over before it had really begun. I felt lonelier than ever.

As I stared out my window that night, the universe remained indifferent and the stars glinted coldly. It felt as if there was nothing but an infinite, cruel void. Perhaps loneliness was my fate, no matter how hard I tried.

Eventually I pulled up the covers, wrapped my arms around myself, and wept for hours. The next morning, I awoke to blue but chilly skies. I told my mother what had happened, and she called in late to work.

I'd lost not only a friendship but also my virginity. I hadn't wanted it to be like this; I wanted a loving boyfriend who would be there for me and vice-versa. If only I could find a partner like me, one who was free and open, I would be complete and loved.

I didn't go to school for weeks. The shame in Andrew's reaction was, for me, exactly why things had to change in our society, and why I would become an activist.

THE AMBER CROSS

In time, the initial sting of my experience with Andrew numbed. But the deep, gnawing desire for connection didn't. Months later

I met Vlad through a chat room for gay teenagers. He attended my neighboring school, and we began a relationship. Vlad was unique, with a sensitivity and maturity beyond his age. He had been a ballet dancer and always stood with perfect, confident posture.

One day of our time together is engrained in my memory forever. My train to meet him slowed at the station platform with its habitual clunk. The doors flung wide, and the smell of burnt rubber hit me, and the cries of schoolboys rushing to take their seats filled my ears. The blue and red of their jerseys blurred as I peered through the crowd, where Vladimir was waiting at the end of the platform. As I ran up the last few stairs, I could see him waving at me to hurry. I just made it. We got on together just as the train doors closed.

I was relieved to finally be done with the school term, and excited for time alone with Vlad. As we filed to the end of the train, we decided to get off at the next station, near our favorite hangout spot. This area of the suburbs had leafy parks where we could escape from view. I had to keep reminding myself that Vlad, my first real boyfriend, hadn't come out yet.

"This weekend I'm seeing my father," Vlad explained. "He wants to take me to the Orthodox church. We have a feast day, and my grandmother's going to cook Russian dumplings."

"That's nice, but isn't your dad a complete homophobe? I thought you weren't seeing him since your parents divorced."

"My father is just *Russian* about homosexuality," he said quietly as some boys from our brother schools rushed past us. "It's like something he's allergic to." He brushed his hand against mine, and his blue eyes shone as we walked.

"How can you go to a church that hates you? I would be so angry with my dad if he were a Christian," I said as we made it up the station stairs. The spring sun shone over the park, and the scent of freesias and freshly cut grass was on the breeze.

"Being Russian is more complex than that, David. Church is a part of our identity. I don't agree with my dad, but I love him," Vlad said.

I shook my head. "I don't like anything traditional like that, Vlad. Christians are bigoted. I mean, I'm spiritual but the Bible's just horrible. I can't stand how ignorance can shroud itself in religious ceremony. Why would a supposed God of love create us with these desires and then punish us for them? Even if Jesus never said anything about homosexuality, God made it pretty clear. I really think it comes back to Paul, who clearly had issues with women and gay people . . ." I trailed off, realizing I'd lost Vlad's attention and that he had found a place to sit down.

After looking to see if the coast was clear, he pressed his finger to my lips and then kissed me. "I have a gift for you," he said, pulling a small pouch from his duffle bag. He dropped it in my hand and smiled proudly. Opening it, I discovered a fine silver-chain necklace with a small amber cross. I held it up and watched as the amber's golden flecks glinted in the sun. It was a mysterious but beautiful symbol.

"My father gave it to me when I was a child. I've been thinking about giving it to you for a long while," Vlad said. "It's just a little token of faith, something to carry on you."

I pulled him in to kiss me. I had met an equal, a true companion, someone who wasn't going to run off, who wasn't afraid of deeper things. Something about him fit, even if I thought his faith naive and misplaced. As we kissed, a sense of security filled me.

Suddenly a weight thudded against my rib cage, knocking

me sideways. Pain pulsed through my right side. In my peripheral vision, I saw something land at my feet in the grass. I looked down, stunned.

It was a large rock.

Vlad's face went red with shock. Wincing at the pain, I looked behind me and saw a man with a white helmet. He flicked his visor down over his face and mounted his motorcycle. As the low growl of his throttle pierced the air, tears of both rage and sadness streamed down my face.

Instinctively I touched the amber cross still hanging around my neck and over my white oxford shirt. Somehow it both confused and comforted me.

GRACE FORETOLD

One of the cafés I liked the most was nestled in the heart of one of Sydney's inner city suburbs, Newtown. The walls were covered with organized sections of books, poetry being my favorite. Posters littered the notice board, including three for a marriage equality march.

It wasn't that long after that day in the park with Vlad. I was meeting up with my best friend, Emma. As I entered the café and ordered my usual soy chai, I looked around but barely recognized her. Her hair had been dyed black. "Hey! What have you done to your hair?"

Emma put down her book. It was my favorite biography of Jean-Paul Sartre and Simone de Beauvoir, one I'd picked up at a writer's festival. "I'm sick of being valued just for my blond hair. It's my statement for the cause of women!" she said enthusiastically.

I smiled and sat down. "Love it. So *you're* the token feminist and *I'm* the token gay activist. Is that how this is gonna play out?" We laughed.

"I actually just dyed it for fun; the protest is secondary," she said with a flourish of conscience. "Also, I'm doing a part for a theatre piece, and it fits with the character."

She leaned toward me. "So, you know how yesterday we were talking about getting in touch with our spiritual side? I saw a sign for psychic readings down the road. Have you ever had your cards read? I'm kind of curious. Want to go?"

I thought of my past obsessions with Wicca and new age religion. I now considered myself an atheist, but I figured there was no harm in a simple reading. We walked down to the health food store, and as we entered, the pungent smell of vitamin tablets, dietary supplements, and patchouli oil filled our senses.

I strode up to the counter, where a woman with dreadlocks tied up in a bun was sitting, filing through the day's receipts. "Could we please have our tarot read?"

She looked at the clock. "Sorry, there's only one reading left for today. I can arrange it for one of you in about fifteen minutes. It's twenty dollars for thirty minutes."

Emma was happy to go another day, so we waited for my reading. I was filled with nervous excitement. When it was time, I passed through the beaded strands that hung in the doorway, clicking exotically together.

A rosy-cheeked woman with dark hair and a large, purple velvet coat greeted me. Sandalwood incense filled the room; aromatic candles flickered in the background. The fragrance was effusive and intense but pleasant.

"Nice to meet you, David. I'm Rose," she said. "Let's begin."

We sat down at the table. She looked into my eyes for a moment, then pulled out her deck. Shuffling it, she placed the deck facedown on the table, and then drew tarot cards from the top, placing them faceup in front of me until a full reading had been laid out. I was skeptical, almost amused by the spectacle. *People believe in this stuff? I mean, it's fun, but . . . seriously?*

Rose inspected my cards. She seemed to be consulting a spirit guide in the form of a Native American sketched on a paper next to her. Suddenly, she looked at me in amazement.

"Incredible! You are very blessed! I need to tell you this now. You are a child of the light, destined to be with the greatest mediator in the spiritual realms, Jesus Christ. He has chosen you!"

I was a bit glazed for the rest of my reading, not really listening to her half hour of babbling about the various cards laid before me. *Jesus Christ?*

Back at the café, I fumed. "Emma, I think that medium is actually an undercover Christian evangelist."

She sipped her latte and cackled. "Uhhh . . . *what?*"

"She said I was destined to be with *Jesus.* I don't think she knew who she was talking to!"

"Maybe she's right, David," Emma said matter-of-factly.

I made a face. "What do you mean? There's no way I'd ever become a Christian. Mark my words. She's a con artist."

"I used to be a Christian," she said. "Maybe it's true, Dave?"

I shook my head furiously. "I hate Christianity."

The next week, Emma returned to have her cards read. Rose never mentioned anything to her about Jesus.

The God who I thought hated me still haunted me, even through a fortune teller's words. And it wouldn't be the last time I wanted God to leave me right alone.

CHAPTER 5

THE GAY WORLD

> There is a way that appears to be right, but in the end it leads to death.
>
> —*Proverbs 14:12*

My teenage years passed, and at last I could put the all-boys school behind me. I often had moments of realization that I was finally free. My university years stretched out ahead, full of possibility. I immersed myself in this new world of student politics and activism, delighted to find a community I could fully belong to.

University felt like safe territory as an open and out gay man. At this time, I began calling myself queer after studying queer theory, which at its heart was about representing the voices not heard in mainstream culture or on the margins.

The political party I was involved with organized a huge rally for marriage equality, and we marched across the Sydney Harbour Bridge. Bedecked with glitter, I held a placard with the words "All love is equal" in one hand and a megaphone in the other. Shouting, "Shame!" at the small group of Christians holding homophobic signs thrilled and empowered me, and my friends and I snickered as we paraded victoriously past those "ignorant idiots." It was one of the greatest moments I'd had since coming out.

My student political faction had also been working nonstop to support a new bill that would legalize and recognize same-sex unions in the Australian Capital Territory and pave the way for nationwide gay marriage. This would mean full legal equality, and eventually societal acceptance, for our relationships. Predictably, Christian political groups were actively blocking this legislation. They had their rights. Why couldn't we have our own?

Weeks before our impending victory, I found out my mother was closer to becoming a Christian. Again I told her she had to choose between the God who hated me and her son. Was my own mother going to sacrifice her love for me to become a conservative?

When Christian people told me they were against same-sex marriage, it enraged me. I believed the Christian God was a moral monster who had punished his son on the cross as an act of divine child abuse. He had become a weapon in the hands of homophobes, used to deprive LGBTQI people of their rights.

Every time a Christian mentioned traditional marriage or even commented on homosexuality, all I heard was hate. The words "homosexuality is a sin" meant we couldn't have a relationship with God or a romantic companion, the two sources of human meaning and happiness. It was as if we were being stripped of dignity and deleted from existence. Anyone who thwarted our access to full acceptance was our enemy.

At last the bill went through. The LGBTQI community was known for having exhilarating parties, and the party to celebrate our victory, held at my friend's terrace house, was no exception. All different types of people from the gay political world were present, from young clerks working for inner-city ministers, to partisan hacks who spent their time constructing the next political stunt, to affluent professionals who used politics as a dating service, to queer activists who often came from less privileged backgrounds.

That night, one of the partisan leaders expressed interest in me. I didn't reciprocate, but his advance gave me the kind of power I desired within the party. Even as I told him off, I was repulsed by the power-hungry person I was becoming. There was something harsh and hard and foreign creeping into my heart. Was this really who I wanted to be?

MARDI GRAS: PARTIES AND PARADES

Pushing doubts aside, I continued to embrace my growing role in the gay activist community. When I turned eighteen, as a rite of passage, my queer friends signed me up to be a Mardi Gras parade official. This was the night our community took over Sydney and celebrated the freedoms we'd won. We sent the clear message, "We're queer, and we're here to stay!"

This event also honored LGBTQI people who had been horrifically treated throughout Australia's history, and those around the world who had been treated as criminals, abused, locked in shame and darkness, or even executed. (Today, in seventy-four countries around the world, homosexuality is still illegal, and in twelve of them it is punishable by death.[7]) But one day we wouldn't have to live in fear.

I counted the days until the parade. A journalist I had been chatting with online told me he'd be waiting at the after-party, and I hoped I might find both emotional connection and an intellectual equal. On nights like these—celebrations of the right to love who we loved—I always planned a romantic conquest.

Lately, I often stayed at different guys' places on weekends, though most of the time I didn't want sex. I didn't like to sleep around, considering what I'd learned about HIV/AIDS and the tragedy it wreaked in our community. To me, promiscuity had nothing to do with being gay. I craved company and intimacy. I believed that one day my search would lead to the committed, monogamous relationship I dreamed of and so fervently wanted.

The day of the parade, I was given a huge water pistol to ward off crowd members who attempted to climb the railing and join the floats. I watched the first float, "Dykes on Bikes," move into place to inaugurate the parade. The sound of cheering and official whistles filled the air as the lesbians led off. To my right, a gaggle of drag queens tried to jump the barriers and join the next float. I blasted them with the water pistol I had been given, washing them down as they laughed and shouted obscenities, mascara streaking their faces. *I'll never forget this,* I thought, laughing hilariously.

The onlookers' cheers were electric as they thanked us for keeping the parade safe. This smooth operation was proof that gay people were no different from the rest of the world. We were human too, a colorful explosion of diversity, and capable of peacefully celebrating our humanity with all its faults, strengths, beauty, and ugliness.

Marching down the street, I was filled with joy, as if a weight had fallen off my eighteen-year-old shoulders. I felt free from all those years of constant questioning. I was gay and proud of it. I had accepted myself.

When the parade ended and the after-party was about to

begin, I suddenly remembered that journalist. He'd texted me, saying he was waiting for me in the dance hall. I entered the huge warehouse, lit up with strobe lights and pulsating with chest-thumping house music. Thousands of gay men with gym bodies were dancing shirtless, a sea of exuberance. At first I was gleeful, but as I watched this moving mass of bodies and saw men locked in lustful embraces, I felt on the outside somehow. *Are these my people?* I asked myself. *Is this what it means to be gay?*

This was the tension I always felt when I was in settings like this. Was being gay just about having a sexual thrill or casual fling, or was there a deeper meaning? To me, being gay wasn't just about sex; it was about a common experience within a community. And this party somehow felt disconnected and impersonal, without the personal acceptance that being gay meant to me. This didn't feel like what I wanted.

I pushed back these thoughts and pressed through the sweaty crowd, still looking for the journalist. The strobe lights flashed, blotching my eyes. I just wanted to get out of there.

I looked and looked. Finally, after an hour, I spotted him, kissing a man with muscles like those of a Greek statue. He saw me staring at him, then turned away, locking eyes with the other man. I left, stung, with doubts I hadn't had when I walked in.

The joy of the parade was soured by a deep pang of ambivalence. *There has to be more to being gay than this.*

"WHAT IS LOVE?"

That doubt would rise and fall like the tides in Sydney Harbour. My search for a deeper love took me to even more adventurous places. Not long after Mardi Gras, I found myself in the heart of Sydney's gay and alternative scene, at one of its most celebrated clubs on Oxford Street. All of Sydney's intellectuals, fine arts students, and writers were there. The guest list was exclusive. I recognized some of the faces from political meetings on campus. One person I knew, an actor I'd dated for a while, avoided eye contact.

A small bar served cocktails named after literary figures, and the sound of the band next door filled the room. Everyone's eccentric clothes—ranging from period costumes to rockabilly outfits to casual drag—blended with the music as people danced.

I used to carry a small journal with me for occasions like these. I would write a philosophical question or the stanza of a poem and pass it around to see the response. Never a dull moment with that journal circulating in a room like that! The question I had tonight was horribly cliché, but one I genuinely wanted an answer to: "What is love?"

The music drew me to dance in the middle of the crowd. I watched as my journal circulated the large sidebar space where everyone was either sitting with a cocktail or enjoying the beats. After hours of dancing, I took my journal back from a girl with a white-powdered face who was dressed like Virginia Woolf. I sat on a couch to regain my breath. Opening the Moleskine journal, I saw a myriad of responses in every kind of handwriting imaginable. Most were superficial or humorous, some deliciously explicit, others deeply jaded—to the point of heartbreak. Many people had sarcastically scrawled, "Baby, don't hurt me." A few were philosophical and flowery, including a quote from Proust and one from Plato. But no one had a real answer. Not really. It was a simple question. Was that room as lost as I felt? Those pages showed nothing but an empty abyss, and I wondered if anyone really had an answer that would satisfy.

As the bass thudded and the crowd laughed and danced, I felt a cry of indignation rise within me. In all our films, songs, and art, we worshiped love, but no one could define it. *Really? This is it?* Maybe no one did know. Maybe no one could know. Maybe in the end, we *were* just slaves to our biological impulses, cultural aspirations, and desires for fame, attention, and company. Maybe love *was* just a game of illusions in a reality of "blind, pitiless indifference."[8]

Years later I would read C. S. Lewis's words that describe what I experienced: "If I find in myself desires which nothing in this world can satisfy, the only logical explanation is that I was made for another world."[9] But that night those words were not there for me. The world around me seemed completely vain.

I started to sense that there *had* to be a higher love that corresponded to my desire for intimacy. Leaving the club, I felt the facade begin to crack. I was losing my faith in the secular world. The war to find love still raged within me, but I knew there had to be more than my incessant search for intimacy in relationships. It just didn't satisfy any longer.

CHAPTER 6

UNIVERSITY AND THE LOVE TRIANGLE

Come, let's drink deeply of love till morning; let's enjoy ourselves with love!

—*Proverbs 7:18*

Autumn leaves skittered across the pavement as I strode through the concrete corridors. They felt like canyons in the urban jungle of my university campus where buildings rose like old-growth rain forest petrified into gray stone. I was returning from an editor's meeting for the student newspaper, where we had decided to feature the gay marriage march I was helping to organize.

My blue shirt read, "We Demand a Better Future" across the chest. Though my bag was heavy with research books and posters, my heart was light. I was grateful to be part of the growing equity and diversity board which ensured the LGBTQI community's safety on campus. The meaning I found in that community and in activity on its behalf overshadowed the nagging doubts I'd felt a few weeks before.

But as I walked past the student commons, I stopped. The Christian Union had plastered their posters over others on the university's main notice board. Just that week, I had read about the mental health of LGBTQI youth from religious backgrounds. I grabbed a staple gun and my stack of marriage march posters, which I had picked up as a leader of the campus Queer Collective. I covered every pastel blue Christian poster I could find. When I finished, I looked over the new rainbow additions to the campus bulletin boards and felt a sense of justice. It was as if I had erected a sign for passersby, declaring LGBTQI liberation from Christian oppression. These little acts of activism, I was convinced, would eventually erode away homophobia and irrational religion. *It's the little things that count, right?* I thought sarcastically.

I frequently made it clear that evangelical or conservative Christians were my enemies, and I avoided them in classes or at parties. Whenever I saw Christians handing out free food on campus or huddled in their pathetic Bible study groups, my skin crawled. I hated their constant effort to indoctrinate me with the deluded notion of living forever with a first-century Jewish carpenter.

But today I had happier thoughts to consider. When I returned to the main campus building, the glass doors swung wide and I saw my friend Michael, whom I'd met through an LGBTQI community website. We had become good friends and intellectual companions, often discussing our views on atheism and philosophy.

Michael's boyfriend of three years, Samuel, was a fashion designer in training. All three of us had become close, and I would often stay over at their pad in the inner city, playing late-night basketball at the park near their house. This particular weekend, Samuel had invited us to his mother's cottage in the Blue Mountains for an escape from the fast pace of Sydney life.

"Ready for the mountains?" I asked Michael, excited. He was wearing his denim jacket and desert boots and had his bag packed.

He smiled. "Definitely! Great news—Sam is coming with us on the train." I smiled widely. I couldn't wait to get away, just the three of us.

ESCAPE TO THE MOUNTAINS

A canopy of mist hung over the gum trees and shrouded us as I got off the train with my two friends. Samuel was wearing a sheepskin jacket, and his blond hair was set in a curled coif; Michael's light brown hair was shaved short. They held hands, sharing a peck on the lips. Michael laughed as Samuel did one of his spot-on celebrity impressions. I laughed too. These guys were the *best*. I hardly felt like a third wheel at all.

Clouds enveloped us as we climbed down the hill from the station to a wooden cottage affectionately named Bunny Hollow. The house, hidden between gum and wattle trees, sat on a slope with open views of the valley's blue vistas. Samuel showed me the guest room and introduced me to his mother, who greeted me with a warm smile.

"David, it's so wonderful to meet you!" she said, beckoning us into the kitchen for some tea. "Samuel tells me you're going to France next year?"

"Yes. I'm doing the same program Michael did in Italy."

"Where?" she asked as Michael left for the veranda with his tea.

"Strasbourg. To study political science," I said. I couldn't *wait* to leave Australia. We chatted pleasantly about Europe and travel.

Finally, I looked around. "Where'd Michael go?" I said to Samuel as his mum left the kitchen.

"He's not feeling very well." Samuel sighed. "He gets in these dark moods. There's nothing I can do." Then he abruptly changed the subject. "I always wanted to ask, could you teach me French?"

I smiled at him. *"Oui!"*

As we talked and joked, he sipped his tea. I studied him. Sam was handsome, with a strong nose and unruly hair. There was a curl to his lip that gave a certain symmetry to his face. His stubbly beard was well kept, and he always dressed stylishly, revealing his creativity.

"Before that, I have something to show you down at my mum's art studio," Samuel said. "I've been keeping it a secret from everyone but her."

I should have gone to check on Michael, but I chose to follow Samuel. Ahead of me, he strode down the grassy hill in his brown Chelsea boots. We stopped at a small shack with a corrugated iron exterior. Entering, I saw that in the back were large glass windows that looked out over the mountainous valley. I turned to my right, and my eyes met an array of drawings and designs of couture. I knew Samuel had been to Hong Kong weeks before to collect fabrics, but never did I expect that his new line would be ready so quickly.

Every design was dazzling, sweeping vividly, with staggering contrasts between sharp oriental lines and organic curves. It was like a symphony for the eyes. As I observed each design pinned on the wall, I spotted a line from one of my poems that I'd shown

Samuel last term. He'd written it in large letters on his design board! I was flattered.

"David," he said, turning to face me, "you're the most fascinating person I've ever met. I love everything you say and write." He paused. "I made this collection for you." He hesitated, then fingered some of the designs. "You were my inspiration. There's such an energy between us. It's driven so much of what I've designed since we met."

His collection was the most beautiful thing anyone had ever made for me. I was speechless. He hugged me, and I thanked him for showing me.

But as we made our way back to the cottage, the air seemed to grow chilly, the valley turning darker somehow. *He's in love with me,* I realized with a jolt.

The table was prepared for dinner, and Michael was stoking the fire next to it. I sat down as Samuel's mother brought out a piping-hot casserole. The fire crackled, and I opened a bottle of peppery Shiraz to pour myself a drink. Watching the deep red wine run down the side of the glass, I knew a war was waging in my heart. My conscience told me that allowing feelings to develop toward my best friend's boyfriend was wrong, but my heart told me to go for what I wanted. And I wanted Samuel.

As I put my glass down, I felt Samuel's foot touch mine under the table. Michael was quietly sitting next to him. I was thrilled with excitement but filled with deep shame. I needed to leave, and quickly, before anything further happened.

But somehow it didn't matter. In our hearts, it had been done. I knew I cared more about my desire for Samuel than I did for Michael, even as every rational impulse was telling me to flee. Still, I summoned all my resolve, packed my bags for Sydney, and departed on the train the next morning, leaving behind some half-hearted excuse by way of explanation.

SEEING THROUGH "LOVE"

A war between conscience and heart continued to rage within me for the next month.

As I wrote a screenplay for my performance classes at university, my dreams were filled with longings for Samuel. I imagined myself sitting with him at fashion shows, traveling the world as I wrote and he designed. *This is so wrong, David,* I thought.

One balmy summer's night, Samuel sent me a message asking me to meet him at Hyde Park. He had news to share.

After I spotted him by the fountain, he told me he'd broken up with Michael and the coast was clear. We kissed. I felt an incredible freedom after a month of being unable to stop thinking about him. Under the fig trees, we lay for hours in each other's arms, staring up at the skyscrapers above us and the blue-grey sky beyond.

As we lay there, the beat of his heart almost lulled me to sleep. Still, I sensed a paranoia in him that made me suspect that things weren't what he told me. To cover it over, he explained why he had broken it off with Michael. *Surely, it's fine,* I thought. *They're no longer together.*

I guessed then, and later found out, that Michael blamed me for the breakdown of their relationship. In reality, I was the catalyst, but not the sole cause, of their breakup. It didn't matter, though. I'd drunk from a cup that was not mine, and even if I didn't want to acknowledge it, it felt as if I'd betrayed Michael.

Weeks passed. One night, as I sat on my balcony, looking back over that view of the floating city, a message appeared on my phone: "I need to see you."

Samuel waited for me in the Italian quarter of Sydney. I jumped out of the cab to meet him at a small art house cinema, where I convinced him to watch a new film by Woody Allen, who was fast becoming my favorite screenwriter. The whole premise of *Vicky Cristina Barcelona* was a love triangle, centered on two holidaying American women who spend a summer in Barcelona and meet a Spanish artist, Juan Antonio, who becomes their mutual love interest. It was uncannily similar to our scenario.

Abandon yourself to the momentary happiness of romantic love, no matter the cost, seemed to be the film's message. At one point in the film, Juan Antonio muses, "Life is short, life is dull, life is full of pain, and this is the chance for something special." *The universe or fate is speaking to me,* I said to myself. *I just need to give in and enjoy what I've found with Samuel.* It was time to throw off my moral bridle. Michael and Samuel weren't together anymore. So why did I feel as if I were betraying one of my closest friends?

Samuel kissed me behind the cinema in the summer heat. "Want to come to my place?" he asked as thunder sounded in the distance.

"Yes," I said, taking his hand.

We turned the corner past the eucalyptus trees above the old park where the three of us used to play basketball. Their branches swayed in the gust, and then cracked when the wind grew stronger. We hurried, and as we reached the door to Samuel's corner terrace, the summer rain fell torrentially, pushing us into his flat, where we kissed under the sound of it.

I woke the next morning in Samuel's arms. It was cold.

I reached for my phone. It was 6:00 a.m., and the sun had barely started to rise. I silently pulled together my clothes and possessions, then glanced back at Samuel. He was lying peacefully, his arms and hands splayed open where I had been. As I looked at him, something broke inside me. I knew something about this wasn't real.

Since coming out at fourteen, I had been looking for value in romantic love. I was weary of the search. With what I had done to Michael, I knew I could never see Samuel again, at least not this way. My guilt consumed me. All I could think of was that I had gotten exactly what I thought I wanted, and the price was a friend. For a moment, I just stood there. Samuel's designs lay strewn around the floor of his studio. Then I turned and left, closing the door we had opened the night before.

The ride home in the back of a cab felt like forever. As I watched the light rain hit the window, a deep exhaustion came over me, accompanied by suffocating frustration and tears. After countless relationships—some faithful and loving, others broken by unfaithfulness—I was tired. I knew my own weakness. My self-made ethics were powerless against my heart and its desires.

I was starving for intimacy, and yet no matter the situation or person, I couldn't fulfill my need. I thought of all those who turned to drugs or casual sex or other vices, and for the first time I understood why.

The pain in my heart was drawing me back to what I termed spirituality. Looking back, I realize my orphan heart was crying out for the love of its Father. But right then, all I knew was I needed to find some source of higher meaning.

CHAPTER 7

CHRISTMAS CONFLICTS

Then you will know the truth, and the truth will set you free.

—*John 8:32*

We should note this curious mark of our own age: the only absolute allowed is the absolute insistence that there is no absolute.

—*Francis Schaeffer*

The hot summer weather woke me early on Christmas day. Stretching my arms, I paused to look out from my balcony at the harbor before getting ready for Christmas lunch. Even though getting through the day's festivities would likely be a chore, I felt optimistic. Memories of Samuel, and my second year of university, were now behind me.

Gatherings were a big affair on both sides of my family, but always more raucous on my father's Greek side. Inevitably, the topic of religion would come up. We were, after all, an anglicized family with none of the Greek customs but all of the stereotypical traits, including passionate debate over politics, philosophy, and religion.

I arrived slightly late and was ushered to the long dining table to find a place among the platters of turkey, prawns, and smoked salmon. My short Greek grandfather and my grandmother were also still chatting with others near a Christmas tree covered in tinsel. They wrapped up their conversation to take their seats. To my dismay, the only spot left at the table was across from my Christian relatives.

I felt a pang of dread. Aunt Helen and Uncle Brendan had minded me from a young age with my parents at work, but I resented their family because of their strongly held Christian faith. I hadn't been to their place in years.

I still vividly remembered my phone conversation with Aunt Helen when she said, "I want to explain why homosexuality isn't a God-ordained lifestyle choice for you, David. I accept you and love you as a person and a family member, but I have to tell you what's true."

Her words felt like a dagger. They were ignorant of the fact that being gay is not a lifestyle choice but an important aspect of who someone is. I had exploded back with a fury that shocked me afterward. "You mad bigot! People like *you* are responsible for the suicide of thousands of gay youth!"

Years later I came to understand that like many Christians, my aunt had used the wrong words to communicate both her stance and her concern for me. My uncle Brendan also deeply cared for gay people. But in my mind, he and Helen were still bigots. Anyone who disagreed with me or had a different vision of marriage was automatically a bigot. No qualification needed.

But on this Christmas day, I took my seat, trying to rise above their hatred. *I'll just ignore them,* I thought.

As we ate, I talked with my cousin next to me. Suddenly I

overheard Uncle Brendan mention God and something about truth. *Truth* was a dangerous word. Through my university lectures, I had adopted the key doctrine of the postmodern worldview: there are no absolutes. Such "truths" are just ways to control other people.

"Are you kidding me? There's no absolute truth and certainly no God," I proclaimed, breaking up the conversation around me. All my relatives stared at me, and the whole room went silent. Out of the corner of my eye, I saw Aunt Helen recoil at my assertion.

"I've studied postmodern philosophy. I can tell you there is *no* absolute truth," I told my uncle. "You can't even communicate truth with language, so please don't try to talk to me about God. It's ridiculous, a delusion. You can't have an exclusive claim to know God. I have many atheist, Hindu, and Muslim friends. Do you *really* think they're all going to hell because they don't know your Jesus?"

"David, there are a few issues with what you are saying," Brendan said, cutting through my exasperation.

"Like what?" I asked irascibly.

"You say, 'There is no absolute truth' as if it is an absolute truth, and you also used language to communicate that. You just doubly contradicted yourself," he said.

He glanced at my aunt. "For me and your aunt, the truth is a Person we know, not just a concept in our heads. He's someone we have a real relationship with." He turned back to me. "Just because our understanding of him isn't always perfect doesn't change that he's the absolute truth. It's his perfect grace, not 'perfect' knowledge of God, that saves us, David."

I pushed my plate away. "But what about all the evil the

church has done to LGBTQI people? Do you really think I'd believe you after all of that?" I shook my head. "I can't believe 'God' would create us this way and then punish us for it. And what about all of the other religions? You haven't answered me. Do you really think half of humanity is destined to hell because they haven't heard of Jesus?" I stood up to leave.

My aunt and uncle also left soon afterward. Years later I learned that on the way home, they talked about my response.

"When David was talking, I saw the Holy Spirit over him. He's going to be saved and baptized with the Spirit in three months' time," Brendan told my aunt confidently.

Aunt Helen stared at him, incredulous. "Are you sure? Didn't you see his reaction?"

He nodded. My uncle wasn't one to push things like prophecy. He was reserved about making extraordinary claims, and yet this time he was *adamant*.

God's grace was reaching out to me in my deepest anger. He had started through my uncle's apologetic witness.

And Brendan was right. One hundred percent.

I had only three months of atheism left.

PART 2

THE ENCOUNTER

CHAPTER 8

EXPERIENCING THE LOVE OF GOD

I have raised up a young man from among the people.
I have found David my servant; with my sacred oil I have anointed him.

—*Psalm 89:19–20*

God waits to be wanted.

—*A. W. Tozer*

It was a busy Friday night, just weeks after my nineteenth birthday. The bridge across Sydney Harbour was packed with cars. From the back of my cab, I looked out over the water and spotted the iconic white sails of the Opera House. Then I lay my head back, relieved to have a break from the monotony of life.

I was worn out from political conferences and late nights spent editing the university student magazine. Instead of the more raucous options available for my night, I decided to go to a small pub to celebrate a writer friend's birthday. It was late March.

As I got out of the cab, the streets were filled with the buzz of Sydney's nightlife. A rainbow flag flew above a building just doors down. I was only a street over from Oxford Street, Sydney's famous gay quarter, which held fond memories of Mardi Gras parades, nights out, and coffee dates with friends.

I walked up the pub stairs and scanned the room. Not many people I knew had arrived yet, but I did spot a friend of a friend holding a drink and sitting alone.

Madeline was a finalist in one of the largest short film competitions in the world, a huge accomplishment for a young creative. Everyone was talking about her in my screenwriting class, and I wanted to interview her for the student magazine. It would easily make the best feature article.

Unlike a lot of my peers, whose creative projects centered on them, Madeline was using her gifts to raise awareness for those often misunderstood or forgotten—people with disabilities. Having a disabled uncle, I found her work inspiring.

As I approached, her brown eyes warmed in recognition, and we said hello. Her hair was cut short, and she wore red lipstick and a black dress. Right away I launched into the question I wanted to ask.

"How did you become a finalist? You just graduated!"

"That depends," she said. "Do you want the *real* answer or the *interview* answer?"

I laughed, unprepared for what would follow. "The real answer, of course!"

"God led me to make the film."

Madeline must have seen the shock on my face. I remembered the conversation with my aunt and uncle over Christmas lunch. *Please don't mention Jesus,* I thought. I couldn't see how

Christianity had anything to do with her work. How could a faith that oppressed me and so many others motivate her to do such good?

"So, which God?" I asked, with a hint of sarcasm. "We talking, like, Vishnu here?"

"Jesus," she said.

A thousand objections flooded me as I thought of this God who stood in the way of my community's progress in society. And yet . . . Madeline wasn't like the other moralizing, intolerant, anti-intellectual, homophobic, anti-feminist Christians I'd met.

She explained that she too struggled with Christian stereotypes and the small-mindedness found in parts of the Christian community. The key word in John 3:16, she said, was *whoever:* "God so loved the world that he gave his one and only Son, that whoever believes in him shall not perish but have eternal life." I realized Madeline didn't see my homosexuality as a hindrance to knowing God. She clearly wanted my community to find the same love she had discovered.

Madeline paused. I knew she had seen that my reaction to her faith wasn't positive. Only my admiration for her work prevented what otherwise would have been a very rude response.

"Do you think there's a God?" she asked. Not a hint of ulterior motive or trying to convert me. Just an open question.

"Well, I'm basically an atheist, but I believe there's a *Something,* I guess. I'm a spiritual person, and I think you have to be blind to believe there's absolutely nothing behind life," I said, looking down at my drink. "I just don't like organized religion. I'm gay, so I know this Christian God isn't an option for me. I've never understood how if he existed, he'd give me these desires, then condemn me."

I expected her to quibble or awkwardly change the subject, like many of my Christian friends. But Madeline didn't hesitate. "David, have you ever experienced the love of God?"

"What do you even mean? No." My only impression of him was that of an angry, distant deity.

"God loves everyone right where they are," Madeline said. I wanted to recoil at her words, yet something drew me deeper.

Suddenly her eyes widened. "David, I can feel God's presence so strongly right now." She paused. "He loves you so incredibly much. I'd never usually ask this, but . . . can I pray for you?"

Instantly I had an internal war over how to respond. *Should I say yes or no?*

A voice in my mind whispered, *You're a good agnostic; you have to be open to prayer, because you don't know if there's a God. Any other response is intellectually dishonest and closed-minded.*

Another thought, this one louder, came on its heels: *Get away from this crazy fundamentalist! She's brainwashed like those Christians you read about in the newspaper!*

The gentler voice won. "Yes, you can pray for me," I said finally. "But I don't think anything is going to happen."

As Madeline laid her hands on me and prayed, the bustle of the pub faded away. I entered into a stillness, a peace. Soon I felt a soft tingling on the crown of my head that slowly intensified, as if someone were pouring oil over me. The warm sensation ran down my entire body like a current of water. It was unlike anything I'd ever felt before.

In a moment, in that experience so totally from outside me, so totally unasked for, everything turned upside down in my mind. All my searching in religion, in relationships, in atheism—none of it compared with this love coursing through me like electricity.

For the first time, I knew God was real and that he loved me. *This changes everything,* I realized.

As my eyes filled with tears, I heard a voice in my head say, softly at first, *Do you want me?* It cut to my core, to a deeper place I never knew existed. It grew in intensity. *Do you want me?*

I'd never heard a voice like this, and I was scared. I didn't know who this was. It felt like there was a dark veil around me, trying to stop me from responding. But I was so stunned by what was happening, and so desirous of real love. I answered the voice, *Is that you, God, Creator of the universe?*

Then again: *Do you want me?* The question was direct and immediate, from outside my own cognition.

A fourth time I heard the voice, this time even louder and more pressing: *Do you want me?*

And I did. I was so exhausted from my loveless world that I reached out for what was offered.

If you are really there, then yes, I said, to my own surprise.

As soon as I did, a laser-like pinprick of light pierced the darkness over my heart and entered that mysterious place deep inside me. I was later to find out that Jesus speaks of this place in John 7:38 as the innermost being, from which rivers of living water, God's Spirit, flow for those who believe in him.

Then I felt a wind, like someone breathing on me, filling me with life. It was as if I were taking my first breath.

"Madeline!" I said, both frightened and exhilarated, "I'm breathing without taking a breath! What's happening?"

"David, that's the Holy Spirit filling you. He loves you," she said, unaware of my internal dialogue.

As she kept praying, I heard the voice ask, *Will you accept my Son, Jesus, as your Lord and Savior?*

Immediately I was offended by the Christian nature of the question. Once again the war inside raged like a tug-of-war over my soul. I heard two voices. The first said, *What you're feeling is a psychological reaction. It's just wish fulfillment! Get away from here!*

A calmer, quieter voice followed it: *I am calling you, David. This is real and true. You've never experienced anything like this in all your searching.* This internal struggle felt like the longest moment of my life. Then the most reluctant of words came from my mouth: "Yes, I accept your Son, Jesus, as my Lord and Savior."

As I surrendered myself, something like hot fire coursed throughout my body. I knew I had become a Christian, and I began to weep.

But these tears were different. They were tears of freedom and healing.

After excusing myself from the friends now celebrating at the pub, I left with Madeline to catch a ride home to my parents' house. In the cab, she attempted to explain what had happened inside my heart, but my mind just couldn't grasp it.

I was dumbfounded. I was an atheist gay activist, perhaps the least likely of anyone to ever find Jesus. But in that moment, I knew I had become a new person.

As I opened the door to my parents' house, I could see the light was on. My mother was up later than usual. When I entered the living room, she saw my face and knew something had happened. "David? Is everything okay?"

I couldn't say it. It was as if admitting what had happened meant I had to eat my words and objections to my mother's faith.

"Mum, tonight . . . I . . . uh . . . think I've become . . . uh . . . a Christian," I said sheepishly. For a minute she stared at me, awestruck.

The moment my news sunk in, she jumped up and hugged me. My mother's reactions always had a hint of drama about them—she had been an opera singer in her younger years. "David, I prayed that if he was truly the God of the impossible, God would save you, because you were so impossible to save! Now I know he can do anything!" she said, wiping away tears.

She told me Aunt Helen had been praying for eleven years that I would come to know Jesus. She also told me about Uncle Brendan's prophecy after Christmas lunch. I quickly did the math and realized that day was exactly three months ago. My salvation had been foretold more than once, it seemed.

I began to see I was the object of a benevolent divine conspiracy to reveal the love of God to me.

CHAPTER 9

THE FILM FESTIVAL

When Paul placed his hands on them, the Holy Spirit came on them, and they spoke in tongues and prophesied.

—*Acts 19:6*

These signs will accompany those who believe: . . . they will speak in new tongues.

—*Mark 16:17*

The night after I met with Madeline, peace washed over me as I slept. It was as if I were dreaming yet somehow aware in semiconsciousness of the Holy Spirit cleansing me, filling me, restoring me from the inside.

As the sensation grew stronger, gushing over me like a torrent, I felt the dead shell around my heart being carried away. Out of nowhere, I began speaking in an unknown language. This otherworldly speech poured out so forcefully that it woke me.

I opened my eyes, realizing I was speaking in tongues. I had read that speaking in tongues was a common brainwashing technique, especially in megachurches. My personal theory was that it helped churches financially exploit people and subdue their rational faculties.

"I'm part of a cult!" I screamed, waking my parents.

"Shhhhhhh!" I heard my father say from down the hallway. He sounded grumpy from being woken. My mother got up to check on me.

"Darling, what's wrong?" she asked, peering around the door.

"Mum," I gasped, trying to slow my breathing, "I think I've become part of a cult!"

"Calm down! What happened?"

I told her what I had experienced while I slept and what awoke me. "Isn't that what cults do?"

She sat down on the bed and rubbed my back. "There's nothing cultish about speaking in tongues. It's pure spirit-to-spirit communication with God. Let me get a Bible so I can show you."

As she left, I thought, *I'm okay with God and Jesus and even the Holy Spirit, but I* hate *the Bible!* It was a book that condemned me and had caused me immense pain. I was deeply skeptical about its composition and historical accuracy. How could it be inspired by the God of love I'd met that night?

When she slipped back through my doorway, I shook my head. "I don't want to read the Bible."

"Wait, let me show you." She opened her well-worn leather Bible and pointed to the page. "It's 1 Corinthians 14:2. Paul explains that 'anyone who speaks in a tongue does not speak to people but to God. Indeed, no one understands them; they utter mysteries by the Spirit.'"

"I hate Paul, Mum! He's anti-gay and anti-women. According to him, you need to be quiet and not teach me anything!"

"Darling, I don't think that's a sound interpretation. And you know, the Bible doesn't just talk about sexuality. It's God's love letter to us." She studied me. "The washing you experienced is described by Jesus. He says in John that for all those who believe in him, living waters will flow from within them."

I couldn't believe my mother knew the Scriptures so well. As she sat next to me on the bed and leafed through her Bible, I was filled with anger. I grabbed it and threw it against the wall.

"I hate that book!"

"David, I'm just trying to help you understand!"

"I'm going back to sleep," I said, turning over.

But even in sleep, I couldn't escape this mysterious presence of God.

Over the next three weeks, everywhere I went, I felt it—him—with me. Whether I was riding on public transport, sitting on a park bench, or attending classes, the same living water flowed through me. Sometimes it was as if a wind unexpectedly blew over and through me.

Strange as it was, I loved this intimate presence. Words could not fully describe the Spirit. Unlike pleasures of this world, there was no adverse effect. Experiencing the Spirit was entirely safe.

I even started sharing the little I'd read about the grace of God with my gay and atheist friends. I just told them what I knew: God offers a free relationship with him through Jesus' death on the cross. He loves absolutely everyone and is desperate for them to return home to him, and it's only in that love that we truly repent.

Christians were amazed by what I knew, even though I'd barely read the Bible since school. My skeptical friends asked me questions I had no answers for, but many were privately interested.

Their questions made me curious about what the Bible said. Cautiously I read portions of it, still avoiding the Old Testament or anything written by Paul. What I did read explained many of my experiences. Gradually I began to see its trustworthiness and value.

But even with all these experiences and my growing openness to the Bible, I struggled to rationally accept God's existence. There was a war between my heart and my mind; my heart knew what had happened inside me, but my mind wasn't convinced. The horrific things the church had done and the pain the Bible had caused the LGBTQI community stood in my way. How could Christians treat gay people that way and yet claim to know the Source of the love I'd encountered? How could God allow hurtful words to be written about gay people and still be good?

I felt myself torn between two worlds: this new Christian world and the gay world that allowed me to be honest about who I was and what I desired. My heart's love for God was growing, but my old loves were still stronger.

Little did I know that God would soon prove himself again in a dramatic way.

A REPLY FROM GOD

The night of the film competition, I set out a picnic blanket near the festival stage. I couldn't wait to see if Madeline's film had won. The atmosphere was electric. A crowd of tens of thousands was gathered around the four big screens in the center of the Sydney city park.

I watched as the orange sky faded into midnight blue, and stars and planets appeared, including Venus, blinking at me from the expanse. Scanning the cosmos, I prayed, *God, if you're really there, I can't just have these experiences. I need a sign, a reply of some kind.*

Soon the competition began. Each film was played, but Madeline's clearly stood out. Its honesty and artistry spoke to me, and judging by the enraptured faces around me, her film spoke to many others as well.

Finally, it was time to announce the winner. Numbers counted down and the suspense grew. The crowd roared with appreciation when Madeline's film won. As the judges hugged her and handed over her trophy, she glowed with joy.

When she stepped off the stage, the press swarmed around her. I ran down to the red carpet, where my favorite Australian actors, Geoffrey Rush and Cate Blanchett, had just walked past. But tonight I didn't care. "Madeline!" I called from the barricades.

She turned and waved her trophy at me. "David, this event is for God's glory. I'm just his servant!" Her face suddenly became serious, and she leaned closer as she shouted, "I need to tell you something! All night, I couldn't shake it. God wants me to tell you he really exists. He's there for you!"

I froze, amazed. The living God had provided a direct reply to my prayer! Perhaps faith really was evidence-based trust in response to real communication from God.

In an instant, I was reassured that God was real, and my heart and my mind were at peace.

"David, I have to go, but come to church with me this Sunday," Madeline called. "I'll give you that interview you've been wanting!"

DIVINE CONSPIRACY

Madeline, I found out, attended the same church movement as my mum and my aunt and uncle. This detail astounded me. When I entered the church with her, the same presence I experienced in the pub flooded back, stronger than before. During the worship time, I stared as people lifted their hands in adoration. I'd never seen anything like it. The Holy Spirit's loving presence emanated out of everyone.

I too lifted my hands. I found it strange and yet natural, as if I were created for it. Floods of power and love flowed over me, and I wept. Jesus' grace had found me in a church—the last place I wanted to be, not long ago.

In his sermon, the pastor quoted Matthew 10:32, where Jesus says, "Whoever acknowledges me before others, I will also acknowledge before my Father in heaven." He followed with a simple gospel message: Jesus died on the cross for our sins to make us right with God, and confirmed it through his resurrection.

The pastor then invited people to accept Jesus as their Lord and Savior. My hand went up straight away, and I walked down the aisle to give my life to him as an outward sign of what had happened to me. As the pastor prayed for me, I repented, turning away from my old life. Even though church culture was still alien to me, I knew I'd come home—to my Father's house.

I basked in God's love and acceptance. But I had questions. *Why did you save me?* I asked Jesus. *Why did you come into my life, when so many others don't know you?*

God was about to reveal his answers to me.

CHAPTER 10

PROVIDENCE AND PROPHECIES

> Today I appoint you to stand up against nations and kingdoms. Some you must uproot and tear down, destroy and overthrow. Others you must build up and plant.
>
> —*Jeremiah 1:10 NLT*

Over the next several weeks, the Holy Spirit did a profound work in my heart as I attended my new church. Incredible as it sounds, some Sundays I saw visions of what I later realized were the heavenly realms.

In one service, I found myself singing, "Holy, holy, holy" entirely out of sync with the rest of the music. Other times, at my first Christian conferences, I began singing songs, sometimes in angelic tongues pouring from my mouth. They were completely different from what was playing, and they were supernaturally beautiful. It seemed unbelievable this was happening to me, but I couldn't dismiss it. I was afraid those around me were going to think I was crazy or something.

Even deeper changes were taking place too. I started to

fall in love with God and told everyone about Jesus. Homeless gentlemen received the gospel message along with fresh sushi, my favorite fast food, on my walk to the station. As I sat next to people on public transport, I felt prompted to speak to them about Jesus' love. I even shared about Christ with some of my toughest atheist and agnostic friends at university. I had no fear.

I read the gospel of John for the first time since my conversion and found I hungered for God's Word. Scriptures began coming to my mind that I didn't even know were in the Bible, and people showed me where they were.

My desires started to change. I no longer felt like hitting up the gay clubs, and my desire for a boyfriend lessened. I felt a deeper desire for fellowship with Christians. Many university classes weren't as interesting to me, and I was frustrated by the anti-theistic tone of most of my professors. The editorial team at the student magazine found my God talk offensive. Many of the members started to withdraw their friendship.

I was a different human being, and it showed. But to my political and gay friends, I was a cultural traitor. I experienced more severe hatred from many of my secular friends than I did before from Christians for being gay. My secular friends assumed things about me that were just as prejudiced, if not more so. Many mocked me. But I knew that before I met Christ, I would have done exactly the same. I could point no finger. I had become the very person I once hated.

Yet despite my longing for fellowship, I was also lonely among Christians. Most of the people around me had no idea what had happened in my life, and those who did were unsure about my still-vocal views on gay marriage.

This Christian culture felt very foreign. As pastors preached, even as I loved what they said about Jesus, I was upset by insensitive things they said about the gay community or by their offhand remarks about political and social affairs. My church was only blocks away from one of the world's largest LGBTQI populations, yet no one expressed any empathy for LGBTQI people or a heart to reach them with the gospel. They seemed to act like they didn't exist, which somehow was more hurtful than vilifying them.

I struggled with bringing friends to church, especially when terms like sin were mentioned flippantly, or when people spoke about how "our values" were under threat, never suspecting that someone with other convictions might be listening. I knew they were talking about people like me, yet there I was, right at the center of this church, by God's own providence.

I often left church distressed, angry, or confused. How was I supposed to be a gay or same-sex-attracted Christian? There were no answers. It felt like I was living a dual existence—my faith on one side, my sexuality on the other.

Yet I knew God understood. I thought, *He who knows all things* must *know how difficult it is for me to belong in the church.* He showed me grace and gave me reminders of his continual, faithful presence. Every Sunday, words and concepts I had been thinking about the previous week seemed to uncannily appear in the sermon, as if the Holy Spirit were saying, *Look, I'm here too. Bear with the church. I'm with you.*

It was the Spirit who kept me there. Each time I attended Sunday services or weekday prayer meetings, his presence filled me like a fire. One Sunday, God's voice was clear: *David, don't worry about the question of your sexuality. Enjoy me. Love me and practice my royal law: love your neighbor as yourself. Your sexuality seems like a mountain to you. It is a grain of sand to me.*

I made a decision to be single for a year to give God time to show me his intention in the Scriptures. *I need to let God be God,* I thought. *After all, if he thinks exactly like me, is he really God, or am I just making him in my own image?* I knew the Bible was clear that God was holy—set apart and different from me, even though I was made in his image.

One Sunday after service, my new friend Sarah and I had a picnic in Hyde Park, at a spot not far from where I'd kissed Samuel just one year before. We spent some time praying for one another. As we sat on the lawn with our Bibles open, it felt like the Holy Spirit came and joined us. When Sarah prayed, she told me she had received a word from God for me. At first, I didn't know what that meant, but I was moved by her care. It was obvious this presence was more than a feeling. He was a person who wanted to speak to us.

There was weight to the words that came next. "David," she said, "you're like a golden chisel in God's hand. You're made to both tear down and build up, like the prophet Jeremiah. Through you, Jesus is going to tear down walls of division in the church and reach many people with the gospel. He's going to take you across the earth to share his love for all people. He's anointed you to do this."

She then read me Isaiah 61:1, which was the chapter Jesus read out loud from at the start of his ministry: "The Spirit of the Sovereign Lord is on me, because the Lord has anointed me to proclaim good news to the poor." Suddenly the sensation of oil being poured over my head in that pub months before made more sense. I understood it more now.

The next week at university, I met with two friends from campus, Stephen and James, a couple planning to be married at their church. I told them what had happened in the preceding weeks, and they invited me to their campus Bible study. Everyone in the study was similar to me intellectually and politically, and many were humanities students. I instantly felt at home. They knew exactly what I was going through, and their affirmation of me as a gay Christian was healing.

We discussed our view that Paul was not aware of the monogamous homosexual relationships exhibited in gay marriages today. I was so relieved and excited by these arguments that I felt a premature reconciliation between my faith and sexuality. It was so encouraging to find friends wrestling like I was. I didn't question what they said, because I trusted their earnest faith and intellectual gifts.

Still, I stood by my commitment to remain single. I was convinced I needed time to let Jesus make his will clear to me.

After all, I considered, *if I'm anointed, he must have something mysteriously great in store for me.*

CHAPTER 11

THE UNRELENTING PRESENCE OF JESUS

> The LORD your God is with you, the Mighty Warrior who saves. He will take great delight in you; in his love he will no longer rebuke you, but will rejoice over you with singing.
>
> —*Zephaniah 3:17*

For my first years as a Christian, I was stuck. There's no other word for it. I felt wedged right in the middle of the church's division over the gay elephant in the room. The root question *Who am I, Lord?* was morphing into *How can I love?* On a fundamental level, I had a practical question to answer: could I live out my Christianity as a partner in a gay, sexually active marriage, or was that in conflict with my newfound faith?

The church didn't make the dilemma easier. *Churches,* I should say, because I attended two of them during those years. One was quite charismatic, its attention fixed on the work of God's Holy Spirit among us. The other was focused largely on social justice.

The pastor of the latter showed me theological arguments

for gay marriage, encouraging me to accept this part of myself actively as a gay Christian man. He spoke about the inclusion of the Gentiles and how throughout church history, many LGBTQI people like me had received the Holy Spirit—proof of their acceptance in Jesus. He explained that I simply didn't have to live under oppressive church laws which privileged heterosexual people. To him, marriage was a bond of love between two individuals, no matter their sex or gender. This union imitated Christ's love for the church and should be offered to all, regardless of their orientation.

However, at this church, the Holy Spirit's presence was somehow *weaker*. It felt different. The same pastor jokingly called me "Jesus-is-my-boyfriend David" because of how I talked about my love for Christ and because I raised my hands during worship, as an expression of my passion and faith. No one else did that there. Most members of the church gave me a cold reaction, dismissive or even condescending, when I described my experiences with the Spirit. In this place where everything in me hoped for affirmation, they were actually affirming only one part of me—the part that was like them, the part they could easily accept.

I also felt uncomfortable with how this church understood the Bible. For them, it seemed useful only to justify their chosen social causes. Jesus was a political zealot, a radical figure who challenged the heresy of private, cheap-grace faith. The cross was a symbol of solidarity with the poor, suffering, and rejected minority groups. They laughed at the theology of the other church I attended. I hated that division and the critical spirit I saw toward members of Christ's body. I didn't see why they couldn't hold on to the best parts of their theology while also, in humility, letting themselves be truly changed by God's Word.

But don't get me wrong: there was also a wonderful side to their faith. I *loved* the way they served the poor and took discipleship seriously in ways many other churches didn't. They did love the heart of Jesus. Just not the whole heart of Jesus, I felt. Ultimately, I realized that the intensity of the first love I'd encountered in the pub was ebbing away faster than I expected it would. And—little surprise—this church really didn't have a category for it.

When I went to the other church with my family, Jesus' presence seemed to come freely, like a flood. The auditorium was filled with loud music and expressive praise. Stage lights flashed, and the worship leaders sang to God as if no one else were in the room. The whole church of more than a thousand people lifted their hands in worship. It was an incredible feeling of joy and oneness. But they missed so much. There was no place in their worship for someone like me, unless I was committed to bottling it all up and becoming more like them, not more like who I most truly was in Jesus.

Still, for all the shortcomings, I felt old mindsets falling away, like the scales that fell from Paul's eyes after his encounter with Jesus. For the first year at my family's church, I wept at every service. I would often shout out in the service when I disagreed with what the pastors were saying, yet I felt power and grace working in me each time I went. Sitting with my mum and Aunt Helen, I was changed by God.

One weekend after the service, I had coffee with my aunt. Despite the ways I saw God moving in my heart, I was irritated with some of the things the church said about homosexuality being a sin. I wanted to tell her my thoughts.

My yearlong commitment to singleness was up. With a deep

internal sigh of relief, I was dating Thomas, a handsome Italian Catholic I'd met online months earlier. He was amazed to meet a born-again Christian who was gay and open to a relationship. But the issue of whether we would be accepted at this church remained. That Sunday, I was ready to reckon with it.

I sat with my Bible open and my coffee untouched. "I can't believe a loving marriage between two members of the same sex is sinful. I'm happy to concede that sex before marriage is wrong, and that's exactly why the church needs to have gay marriages," I said to my aunt. "If I wanted to marry Thomas, where would I go? I'd have to leave this church where God meets me so profoundly." I stared intently at her, waiting for a response.

Helen met my gaze. "David," she began slowly, "I agree with what Scripture says. I believe its intent is clear. But it's *easy* for me. I've never struggled with same-sex attraction."

She paused to sip her coffee before continuing. "All of us have a cross to bear, an ultimate issue to wrestle over with God. This is something you'll have to work out with *him*. That's faith! You have the Holy Spirit, your teacher, living in you now. You need to seek *his* answer to your question. The voices of falsehood are loud—*so* loud. But God's voice is a still whisper. You'll have to learn to hear him. Remember, God will never contradict his Word. Never."

She locked eyes with me. "I'm sorry if we or this church have failed to love you. No one should bear their cross alone. We're here for you. Whatever you come to believe about your sexuality, you are always welcome, and if you have a partner, you're both welcome." She reached across the table and grabbed my hand. "Yes, we have a policy that means our church will submit to what Scripture says about marriage. But, David, if we didn't have you, we would be missing an irreplaceable part of Christ's body. You are wanted."

That weekend, I got a glimpse of what real acceptance looks like. My aunt, the church, and my mother weren't going to change what God's Word said, but they *would* love me, accept me, and embrace me no matter what. Through their responses, I peered into Jesus' acceptance of my human struggle maintaining both truth and grace. I didn't fully understand it. At all. But I knew he was there. I sensed his unrelenting presence. I concluded I would call this church home.

TOUCHING HIS ROBE

As time went on, I started to desire deeper, longer worship than the fifteen-minute segments of praise on Sunday mornings. A friend invited me to a healing service, in which a small group of passionate worshipers and healing ministers from my church gathered to pray for the sick. As we sang and adored Jesus, the chapel was filled with a glorious presence, as if God had come into the room somehow. I had sensed this before during services, but never so powerfully. My heart trembled as both the power of God and the pain of my past washed over me.

I suddenly thought back to the story of the woman with the problem of blood in Luke 8:43–48. Jesus, walking through a crowd, was surrounded by people pressing to see and touch him. A woman who had suffered for almost her entire adult life pushed through, hoping to touch the hem of Jesus' garment.

This woman had not done anything to have this problem. It wasn't her fault, but it meant she was ostracized, deemed perpetually unclean by the law of Moses. While her bleeding and uncleanness was not an exact equivalent to being same-sex attracted, her suffering and predictament reflected mine and spoke to me. The lack of a solution in the Jewish religious system resonated with how I felt about church. I too didn't fit, through no fault of my own. I felt I was continually questioned, looked on with suspicion, or deemed second-class by the crowd around me. The constant feeling that I needed to explain myself exhausted me.

I recalled how with amazing faith, the woman reached out and touched Jesus' hem. Jesus felt the power go out of him in that moment of union, and she was healed. What if what I had been looking for this whole time was the healing of simply being close to Jesus? I sensed myself on the edge of a profound mystery.

The kingdom of God, I realized, is for those who, like this woman, are poor in spirit. It is this very poverty that leads them to reach out for God, longing for him. In this place of trust, we are lifted up, made whole, and brought into the compassionate embrace of Jesus. Could my same-sex attraction be not simply a barrier but actually the *means* to seek greater grace and wholeness in him? Might it bring me close to him in ways that no other work or struggle could?

The worship continued. "Worthy is the Lamb who was slain," we sang. As we adored Jesus and shouted, "Holy, holy, holy!" I felt a presence in the middle of the room. It was overwhelming. So *real.* But I wasn't afraid. I knew it was the Spirit of Jesus. As his presence came over me, my heart opened afresh to God's grace. Tears fell from my eyes as I felt past sins being cleansed by his shed blood.

Reach out and touch the hem of my garment. The voice in my heart was unmistakable. As I closed my eyes, a bright light shone from above. I can't explain it, but I looked up at the dazzling sight of Jesus with his back to me, high and lifted up. *David, take hold of my presence,* he told me. *All you have to do is hold on.*

In the vision, I reached out and touched his robe. It shimmered with light yet had an otherworldly substance; it was anything but flimsy and ephemeral. Power flowed through my hand and through my body as I experienced my own union with grace. I held on.

And somehow I knew that healing had met me and was holding me.

I had so many questions and deep hurts. But in that moment, I chose to simply trust. Jesus called me to step into the unknown, and I knew he would walk with me each step on the difficult road ahead, until I reached the other side of understanding.

He would be there. No, that wasn't it. He *was* there. And I would keep holding on.

CHAPTER 12

THE ROOT OF BITTERNESS

He has sent me to bind up the brokenhearted.

—Isaiah 61:1

See to it that no one fails to obtain the grace of God; that no "root of bitterness" springs up and causes trouble, and by it many become defiled.

—Hebrews 12:15 ESV

As I slid into my seat for a language theory class, our language and philosophy professor leaned over the lectern, his face animated. "This week we'll be looking at Nietzsche's statement 'God is dead,'" he explained. To us, our professor was an intellectual giant, writing for a living and publishing academic articles on modern language theory and poetry.

I was now in my third year at the university, studying culture, writing, and journalism, and it wasn't making holding on to Jesus an easy proposition.

Throughout the lecture, our professor read from European philosophers who had come to the same conclusion Nietzsche had. "Michel Foucault argued that 'the individual, with his identity and characteristics, is the product of a relation of power exercised over bodies, multiplicities, movements, desires, forces,'"[10] he said, pausing to peer at us over his glasses. "Foucault and Lyotard show us that there is actually no such thing as a grand narrative that can claim to be absolute truth; rather *we* construct these narratives to control others. There is no such thing as 'meaning' without a power relationship involved."

I absorbed everything he said. While I was now a Christian, I saw that these thinkers weren't denying the reality of God, just questioning our capacity to know him. They were being intellectually honest. Could I blame them for that? Without the Spirit of Jesus' revelation and his work to communicate with us, God *was* dead to us. Sure, the skeptics ended up in a place few would wish to go. But they were following the truth as they saw it, more honestly than many of the Christians I'd met.

This wasn't the only obstacle I had to overcome since becoming a follower of Christ. Though I didn't realize it, I also had deep bitterness because of past hurts Christianity had caused me. I could not let go of my activist past, especially when I heard of numerous young gay people committing suicide and of the hate crimes committed against LGBTQI people every week around the world. I seethed with anger, and rightly so. *Why aren't Christians standing up for these precious human beings?* I wondered, my heart breaking. Clearly, many people saw homosexuality as something to resist at all costs, even if that cost was a life. People like me were the victims; *they* were the aggressors. That much seemed obvious.

I struggled to forgive the church for its lack of love and understanding for the LGBTQI community. Many of the characterizations of gender I heard inside church angered me. They constantly talked about what I understood as "gender essentialism," the idea that a person's sex is fixed and their gender is in no way constructed. (This book isn't the place to fully deal with this question. For now, let's just say it's complicated.) I saw *almost no* sensitivity for transgender or intersex people. There was no way to account for many of the complex realities of sin and the created goodness of our humanity. In the Christian mind, it seemed there was no nuance to human gender or sexuality; it was just "a boy with boy parts" or "a girl with girl parts." How did this understanding answer the question of intersex people and genetic exceptions? How about those who experience gender dysphoria? Eunuchs in the Bible? The story was much more complex, and even *one* exception to the rule prompted honestly asking why.

I still did not understand the depths of my bitterness, but I was about to take another step in my journey to forgive. The Sunday following my class, I sat next to Aunt Helen. The church was packed, and something seemed different. Since becoming a Christian, I'd frequently heard the word revival, but I didn't really know what it meant and had never experienced it firsthand. Today I would. I sensed in others around me a hunger for God that I'd never felt in the service before. Helen swept back her long black hair and looked at me sideways. "Get ready," she said. "God is about to move!"

As the band played, the lead singer suddenly stopped the usual program. The whole church started to sing three simple words: "I exalt thee!"

I cannot claim to explain it, but again it felt like a power from outside filled the room. As it became stronger and stronger, my chest shook from within. I felt as if my heart were being cleansed. The words from Ezekiel 36 came to me: *I will sprinkle you with water and give you a heart of flesh for a heart of stone.*

As in previous encounters with God's Spirit, pain quickly resurfaced from my past. As I closed my eyes and lifted my hands and voice, I saw a picture in my mind: what seemed to be a thick root, deep in my core. The memories of hurtful things people had said to me, my own anger toward the church, my past relationships and friendships—all these flitted past. *What is this?* I asked.

This is the root of bitterness that defiles many. I recognized this from Hebrews 12:15. Deep inside, rejection had rooted itself as bitterness. My sorrow had grown into darkness and morphed into something strangling my soul. It was a legitimate hurt, to be sure. But it was growing into something monstrous. God needed to pull it from me before it *became* me. All I could do was ask for the strength to surrender.

The worship music crescendoed. A liquid purity seemed to fill me, a spiritual sense of something beyond my understanding. Suddenly I felt as if I were in another dimension yet somehow still present in my body. *Perhaps this is what John referred to as being caught up in the Spirit,* I thought.

As I looked, I saw the whole earth. It was filled with a sea of people doing all the things we know so well: backbiting, swearing, slandering, jeering at God, setting themselves up as his judges. Their hatred was palpable. They were gripped by pain yet filled with rebellion toward the God who could heal it if only they would let him. It was horrific. I felt my heart break for every person in the crowd.

Then I spotted myself among them.

I heard a voice say, *This is what you would have become.* I looked up and saw Jesus, lifted above the earth, shining in unapproachable light.

I opened my eyes and was back in the auditorium. The whole

church started to sing in adoration, "Holy, holy, holy is the Lord." I had never seen a service where every single person was so focused on Christ. The contrast to the people in my vision stunned me.

As I closed my eyes and raised my hands, it happened again. I saw Jesus and the jeering crowd of people. His whole being radiated with energy. The words of Colossians 1:17 flashed through my mind like an arc of electricity: *"He is before all things, and in him all things hold together."*

I heard Jesus say, *David, my son, you are free.* He raised his hand in a gesture of authority, and dazzling light swept the face of the earth. It touched various people in the crowd, transforming them. His voice boomed: *My glory will come for them.*

This light finally touched me too. I let out a bellow of anger. The music wasn't enough to mask it, and my aunt looked at me, startled. But I barely noticed. Something was happening inside.

I felt God's power come upon me. As my chest trembled, this deep root of pain was pulled out of someplace deep within me. Finally, and gloriously, I was free from past injury. My heart had been set free and softened.

Later, as we talked, my aunt saw that I'd been set free from the unforgiveness that kept me from fully following Jesus and trusting the church. Somehow I knew she was right.

The vision had marked me. My bitterness from feeling rejected by Christians and God was removed, replaced with a knowledge of just how deep God's love for this world and for me went.

Just when the path ahead seemed impossible, Jesus turned my bitterness into life-giving joy. The horizon that had felt so stifling—the authority of Christ—had widened into a vista as broad as the world. I realized that this Jesus is forever the exalted Lord of all.

CHAPTER 13

THE GOSPEL OF GRACE

> It is by grace you have been saved, through faith—and this is not from yourselves, it is the gift of God—not by works, so that no one can boast.
>
> —*Ephesians 2:8–9*

My bitterness was gone, but the other war continued in me. I wrestled more than ever with my two conflicting identities, knowing that aspects of my gay identity no longer worked with the new person I was in Christ. The battle exhausted me.

I faced two opposing temptations: one was to try to fit into the church by hiding my real life and history; the other, to make everything about my gay identity, ignoring the call to follow Jesus. I wanted to be accepted by Christians and follow the Bible's ethic, but I also felt that God called me to personal authenticity. *Following Jesus must lead me to honesty,* I thought, *or it would not be following Jesus.* I couldn't imagine the Christ of my vision condoning hiding myself away. His light and power were so far beyond those kinds of mental and cultural games.

I was a Christian. I also was gay. What did that mean? They felt like irreconcilable realities, identities at war. But were they?

Throughout my primary school years, Christianity had seemed like a system of laws, doctrines, oppressive constraints, and social conventions created to try to get right with a God who demanded perfection but could never bring himself to say good enough. I now knew I could not work my way to God, but what did it mean to obey him, to love him with my whole self, from the heart? He had saved me, and I wanted to live a life that met his approval.

As I read Scripture, especially Paul's letters, it became clear that rules could not make me right with God. That was why Jesus Christ came to save me. If I could have become perfect by myself, why would I have needed his salvation in the first place? He was full of grace, giving it richly to all who repent, filling them with the Holy Spirit, and reconciling them with the Father.

Other things I was learning surprised me. I had never known that the gospel stood *against* many of the social constraints or laws of its ancient context, which social groups used to condemn each other. What would this mean if it was true? Might the gospel I'd once considered my worst enemy be an unexpected ally in moving beyond condemnation and hatred?

While the New Testament upheld that the law was perfect, it also taught that the law could never produce real righteousness in us. At best it showed us God's perfection. At worst it turned us into religious fakers, whitewashed tombs. My desire to make myself worthy of God's love was actually working against his grace in my life. But how could I navigate my sexuality through this gospel of grace? The question haunted me, and more than as an abstruse question of theology. It involved my very life.

One day, sitting on my bed, I listened to a Melbourne pastor preach on freedom, looking at letters to the Galatians and Romans. "We are already declared righteous in Christ yet still experience sinful desires," he explained. When we form our Christian identity, we have to understand the difference between obedience by law and obedience by grace. He quoted Romans 4:4–5: "To the one who works, wages are not credited as a gift but as an obligation. However, to the one who does not work but trusts God who justifies the ungodly, their faith is credited as righteousness."

Something clicked when I heard that. Doing good was wonderful. But it was ultimately useless in creating true relationship: "By grace you have been saved through faith. And this is not your own doing; it is the gift of God, not a result of works, so that no one may boast" (Eph. 2:8–9 ESV).[11] *Wait,* I realized. *My sexual orientation has nothing to do with my righteousness before God!* I was accepted by him because of Jesus Christ, not because of my moral performance. I didn't have to earn it. My chosen sexual *behavior*, just like for a heterosexual person, was a different story. But my orientation? It was not a barrier. It was just part of me.

I felt I had been given back something of who I was. Identity and action separated themselves in my mind, and I caught a glimpse of a third option for my life, one I hadn't suspected until that moment.

The false gospel of striving fell like shackles, and I began to see the beauty of grace, and the real gospel of Jesus Christ.[12] Again the truth hit me: *My sexual orientation does not separate me from God!* My sexual orientation had nothing at all to do with this free gift of grace that had been placed in my hands.

Any attempt to obey God through my striving and effort, rather than his grace and power in me, was resisting the Spirit of God. As Paul stated in Galatians 5:1, "It is for freedom that

Christ has set us free. Stand firm, then, and do not let yourselves be burdened again by a yoke of slavery."

I leapt off my bed and shouted for joy. (I know, I should probably be more demonstrative in my emotional life.) "I'm free. I'm actually free!" I felt liberated from the law's condemnation. My desires could not condemn me. *This* was radical, beautiful grace. Suddenly my identity no longer centered on what I desired sexually; it centered on Jesus Christ and his costly and abundant grace.[13]

MISSING GRACE

As with most of my breakthroughs, though, my questions seemed like the Greek Hydra: chop the head off one with a good answer, and two more would grow in its place. If God's Word was so clear, I was confused as to why the church was so quick to emphasize obedience through the law and so slow to offer grace to LGBTQI people (or in some cases, act as if there is no law in the first place!). Rather than inviting the LGBTQI community to know God by first showing them love, churches were often guilty of doing all kinds of irresponsible things, including using the Old Testament law to condemn people's behavior in the most vicious terms. It struck me that this graceless message was deadlier than the world's unrestrained sensuality, because it hindered the *real* good news. It was like inoculating people against the gospel: when the truth came, they would bristle, thinking, *I've heard that before, and you aren't duping me again.*

Historically, the church had more often than not dealt with moral issues like homosexuality by focusing on sin management rather than emphasizing Christ's transforming grace through the Holy Spirit. This only confirmed what many in the LGBTQI community believed: that God wanted to enslave them in an oppressive obedience of hopelessness. He was a thirsty God, in so many minds, who wanted their very lives, their very identity, to appease his wrath and disgust.

And I'd been one of those people, of course. One of my big hindrances to faith was the practice of reparative therapy, for years recommended and used in the church. This outdated science saw homosexuality and same-sex desires as a pathological disease and viewed the production of heterosexual desires as the cure. Problematic on every level—theologically, psychologically, scientifically, clinically. After I met Christ, I resolved never to get involved with a reparative ministry. *If the gospel really does transform us from the inside out,* I reasoned, *it needs no help from a man-made solution. God calls us to walk through our weaknesses in his power, not to try to change ourselves into something acceptable to him.*

Reparative therapies also pointed to a deeper issue. They missed the point that God, not heterosexual marriage, was the goal of our desires. Why would someone give up their same-sex desires and their hope for romance, unless they'd found something higher? When Paul wrote in 1 Corinthians 6:13 that the body is "for the Lord, and the Lord for the body," was he not pointing to a desire even more fundamental than sex? Our deepest longing was to be spiritually intimate with God, to experience the belonging we were made for. Many people in the church, I realized, didn't even have a real, practical category for this belief. At least, they didn't act like they did.

I had committed to a year of singleness not as an act of legalistic obedience but as an act of faith, from a desire to experience satisfaction in Christ. The motivation for this decision came from trusted people who spoke truth and grace into my life. My church never compromised their views of sexuality and the priority of God's presence, even though sometimes that made me angry. I am eternally grateful. Without these clear boundaries, I would have found it far harder to find real repentance and stay on the narrow path of righteousness I now attempted to walk by the grace of Jesus.

A WAY ACROSS

I sat in my car before a job interview, reading Romans 1, especially the bit about same-sex expression. It stung. Grace was making a way. But even after learning so much about it, at times I found myself exasperated. Some of my closest friends at church had either entered romantic relationships or become engaged. Simply put, I was lonely. Watching them enjoy something I was missing out on was hard, especially when everyone around seemed to revel in married bliss as the ultimate experience of human life. Even in my church, friendship seemed secondary to romantic love. It seemed like everyone had been reading Jane Austen more than the New Testament, or watching nineties rom-coms more than the work of the Spirit.

I felt guilty for judging them so quickly. But the struggle wasn't just a problem of pride. As I sat in my seat, I felt so torn between my desire for a boyfriend and God's will. *Lord, how could you allow me to have these desires?* I asked him again.

Nothing.

Apparently, you don't get life-defining revelations on your

own timetable. *God, how can you possibly allow me to go through something this hard?* I thought. *How can you expect me to never belong? To live without a companion, without a family?* I had no doubt that I'd be a faithful husband, a caring dad. I could see myself growing old with the husband I'd never have, raising my kids to love Jesus. For the first time since I met Jesus in that pub years before, I doubted it—doubted it all.

He could have put kind and detailed instructions for this in the Bible. Instead we got a handful of difficult passages that just seem to prompt confusion, hatred, and bickering. My anger grew. This time I yelled out loud, "Lord, if you really cared, why didn't you just tell me what to do?"

As I lowered my head against the steering wheel, I sensed his still, quiet voice. *David, I have concealed this as a mystery that I will reveal on the final day. Right now, I need you to trust me in the unknown. As you keep walking in my grace, I will show you the deeper secrets of my Word. I will not abandon you.*

The Spirit of God was suddenly there with special weight. I felt his strength fill me. I was no longer sitting in the car but seemingly standing at a cliff, with no way across the expanse to the other side. *It's hopeless,* I thought. Far from being encouraging, this was just a visualization of how stuck I was. No explanation.

The next night at a prayer meeting, I had the same experience. Again, in my mind, I stood at that cliff's edge. There was simply no way across.

But this time there was more than silence. This time God's voice whispered, *Walk on nothing. I will hold you up. Do not be afraid. Walk by faith and not by sight. Trust me. Step over.* I closed my eyes in the vision and stepped, straight over the edge. I didn't fall. My foot was held up, by what I could not see. But whatever it was, I could walk on it. Step by step, I progressed across the impossible chasm. Finally, I made it safely to the other side.

This was the precious trust of believing and not seeing everything! This was a deeper, maturing faith! I realized that God held me up when I did not know how to go forward.

I thought back to moments I had found it hard to trust God because of how different the church was from the gay world I came from. The values. The language. The politics. The culture. Yet even though this Christian world was ignorant of what I had been a part of, somehow I knew I was meant to belong here. If I had been given grace, I could show it to others. Could? No, *must.*

The vision came back twice more, each time taking me a little farther. On the other side of the divide, the land was thick with vegetation. I could not see through it. Again it seemed impossible to move ahead. Then I looked down. In my hand was a sword. I could not see the way forward, but I could cut it. *He is making a way in the wilderness,* I realized. The sword God had placed in my hand was the sword of the Spirit. The Holy Spirit would open up the way of grace for me, through the Word of God by faith.

David, God said to me, *I have called you to make a way where there is no way. Many thousands will find their way to me through you. I love you, my son.* I was flooded with a sense of his closeness, even as I pondered his words.

The last time I found myself there was months later. I was again exhausted, struggling to trust God. This time in the vision, I found myself in a pitch-black night, surrounded by thick forest. *Keep going, David,* I heard a voice call, though I could not see who or where it came from. Taking my sword, I hacked my way through the vegetation and entered a clearing. Suddenly a blinding light shone down from a majestic mountain far off in the distance. *You will lead them here to Zion, my heavenly city,* the voice told me.

The dazzling light from the city filled me with hope and gave me strength to keep trusting God when it felt impossible. Jesus filled me with the desire to obey through grace. This was his power in my weakness.

So much was unresolved. So much still did not make sense. While I still believed gay marriage was the way forward for my same-sex desires, I had learned not to try to earn grace but to obey out of it.

Strengthened, I was ready to take another step of faith. Where it would lead me? I had no idea.

PART 3

WRESTLING WITH GOD: SENSE AND SEXUALITY

CHAPTER 14

LIVING UNDER GOD'S WORD

If we come to Scripture with our minds made up, expecting to hear from it an echo of our own thoughts and never the thunderclap of God's, then indeed he will not speak to us and we shall only be confirmed in our own prejudices. We must allow the Word of God to confront us, disturb our security, to undermine our complacency and to overthrow our patterns of thought and behavior.

—John Stott

The Christian story proclaims that all the demands of Scripture are ultimately summons, calls, invitations—beckoning us to experience true, beautiful, and good humanness.

—Wesley Hill

I delight in your decrees; I will not neglect your word.

—Psalm 119:16

I'd been a Christian for three years, and the question of whether same-sex sexual expression was always sinful loomed. I had learned that grace, as Paul said, was not a license to sin. Okay. And I knew the attraction itself wasn't sinful. But what about acting on it? I was still dating Thomas, so this wasn't just a theoretical question.

I was insecure, uncertain, searching. I wanted to start by learning more about affirming theology.

Through my university, I met a new friend, Josh, who headed up a Christian media club. I admired his sharp intelligence. However, I also knew he was part of the denomination I grew up with at school, which sometimes made me defensive in our conversations.

Every week, Josh and I met at a café a few blocks from the university. As I ate my vegan nachos and he sipped his chai, we studied the Bible. Through our discussions, I gained a deeper understanding of the scandalous nature of God's grace, and how the worst sinners and the most moral citizens both equally fall short of his glory. Only Jesus could lead us into glory and reconciliation.

"Hey, David, do you want to come to a Bible conference? I'm going," Josh asked one day.

I shook my head and shifted in my chair, uncomfortable. "Not sure that's my cup of tea. I assume they're all against gay marriage. And is the worship any good?"

"I can't guarantee about the worship," Josh said. "But there's a scholar and Bible teacher coming from Canada—Don Carson.

He's going to talk about the inspiration of the Bible. I think you'd find it helpful." He paused. "Actually, I already asked my church if they would pay your way. So . . ." He smiled.

I sighed but was touched. "And they said yes?"

"Yup."

What could I say?

The day of the conference came quickly. As I entered the huge hall, I spotted many old school friends in the crowd of thousands of young people. I had walked into the heart of evangelical Australian faith, and I was curious and nervous.

When Don Carson got up to preach about the Bible's place in the Christian life, I hung on his words. "We must not put ourselves *over* Scripture," he said, "but we must live *under* the Word of God."

For the next forty-five minutes, he poured out his heart, imploring us to treasure the Bible, God's greatest gift outside of himself. Thousands of saints, he explained, had lost their lives so we could hold it in our hands. How would we receive it?

As he spoke, the Holy Spirit convicted me that I needed to trust God's authoritative words. Tears poured down my cheeks. I realized I had sat in judgment above Scripture, never really appreciating its preciousness. I had never been willing to submit to it. I could no longer claim to love Jesus without *really* knowing his words and choosing to live according to them.

Carson's sermon sent me on a deeper journey of exploring the Bible, especially what it said about sexuality and holiness. This was not a flippant or trivial issue for me. Celibacy still wasn't a serious option in my mind, but I felt a conviction, a tug in my heart. I sought to ignore it; I had so many friends in loving gay relationships.

How could I believe there was something wrong with seeking a monogamous, faithful, same-sex relationship that eventually led to marriage? But after hearing Don Carson, I needed to confirm whether Scripture actually supported—or at least allowed—my position. I desperately needed godly, mature believers who could face my questions and answer them using Scripture, reason, and tradition.

Now that I was uncertain about gay marriage, when I was in secular spaces that believed the church needed to affirm it, I remained quiet, feeling confused. For the first time, the secular world felt unsafe to me. I started to understand what it was like to be an orthodox Christian in a world that quickly judged people according to stereotypes and would not take the time to understand the real complexity of their situations. In a way, that was a familiar feeling, as you can imagine. But it was odd to experience it from this new vantage point.

While I saw that Scripture had lots to say about homosexuality and about marriage, my struggle was anything but simple. I wrestled with what to accept and what to reject, and it all was *achingly* personal. This was about my life, my real life. My choices. My living situation. My hopes. My parents' hopes. All of it.

If I allowed my own biases to fade away so the text could speak for itself, what would I do if it said what I *really* didn't want to hear?[14] I knew I would be rejected by many friends I dearly loved for taking this incomprehensible position. And how could I blame them? By everything we'd ever held as true, I would be betraying them.

Yes, the cost just felt too high. And I didn't really have to decide anyway just yet, right?

Right.

CHAPTER 15

MARRIAGE AND THE CHURCH

The real sin of marriage today is not adultery or lack of "adjustment" or "mental cruelty." It is the idolization of the family itself, the refusal to understand marriage as directed toward the Kingdom of God.

—*Alexander Schmemann*

We live in a world, in fact, in which respect and support for *eros* has acquired the hallmarks of a cult.

—*Andrew Sullivan*

You shall have no other gods before me.

—*Deuteronomy 5:7*

Since coming out at fourteen, I had searched for meaning and transcendence in romance. Now that I'd arrived in the Christian world, I was beginning to find that meaning in a deeper relationship—with God. And yet something just didn't add up.

I saw many of my Christian peers spend more of their time pondering who their future spouse might be than pursuing God. A kind of matrimonial madness seemed to have descended upon everyone—like that scene from Disney's *Bambi,* in which the animals flounced around the springtime meadow, surrounded by pastel flower petals, utterly "twitterpated." It got ludicrous at times. Many of our pastors would occasionally tell single members of the church to stand up, look at each other, and find their future marriage partner. Sure, we all laughed. But still—*what?*

This puzzled and disturbed me. I mean, I had read up on my Christian history. Until the Reformation, most of the superstars of Christianity were single. Why had so many of our forerunners in the early church been celibate, if marriage was the golden ideal of Christian life? The way people talked, marriage was almost as big a deal as getting saved in the first place.

Reminders of it were everywhere—in the programs, in our church planting teams sent out for ministry, in the assumptions that people glibly preached and prayed. I suspect pretty much anyone single in the church today can relate. I felt discouraged.

It was as if the message to Christian singles was, "If you just get married, have kids, and buy a property, you'll be truly happy." I mean, it made sense; no one wants to pay their mortgage alone or come home with the flu to an empty apartment. But it began to ring hollow. It also felt familiar.

Both in the gay community and in the church, what seemed to matter most to people was fulfillment in a partner. Singleness was second-class. The sense of displacement I had felt at the Mardi Gras after-party wasn't that different from what I felt on Sunday. Both situations seemed idolatrous.

Shouldn't only God occupy our sense of purpose? Was our goal really to produce happy, debt-free, middle-class families? I mean, that's great, don't get me wrong. But is that *it?* Then why was Jesus a man of sorrows with no place to lay his head, and single throughout his ministry?

Jesus was an unmarried, childless man in a Jewish society of family values, and a celibate in a Roman society of sexual liberation that mocked singleness. In a world of two-sided sexual obsession, Jesus invited others into pure intimacy, modeled loving friendship, and lived in life-giving singleness.

I never once heard a sermon about the friendship or singleness of Jesus Christ. Why? I wondered if we were missing the point. Jesus called us to value him above everything else, including our sexual desires *and* our marriage relationships. Yes, marriage was God-ordained, and God had said it was not good for man to be alone. But God, not marriage, was to be our *ultimate* desire. Period.

This overemphasis on marriage made it terribly difficult, as a gay man wrestling with my sexuality, to flourish in the young adult community at my church. When the focus was on God's kingdom, I could belong, but as soon as romantic relationships were the focus, I felt alienated. I often wanted to run out of meetings in tears.

My frustration culminated at a men's conference. We were encouraged to invite friends, and I brought two gay friends from university. Both of them sat with me, their disgust apparent at this "heteronormative" nightmare they'd been sucked into. It was *incredible* they had even agreed to come. But I hoped that, like me, they'd discover in the messages the grace of Jesus Christ.

As I sat worshiping Jesus, I thought about how same-sex attractions are not some horrible curse but an invitation to live a radical life that brought about a far deeper faith than many aspired to live. As in the vision of the forest I had to cut through, I had to trust that God would show me the way through my struggle. He would show me what it looks like to follow Christ in my situation. As my mother had told me when I confessed I'd become a Christian, God really was the God of the impossible. Did I truly believe it?

I felt God speaking in my heart and was deeply encouraged. I did believe it. I did.

The good feeling didn't last long, though. My heart dropped as the pastor transitioned out of worship and made a passing joke related to homosexuality. One strike was all my friends could take. They signaled that they were leaving, and, ashamed and upset, I followed them out. As we made our way to the car, the Lord whispered to me, *David, I'm sorry. Remember how much grace I've had for you. Please have grace for the church, my broken bride.*

The drive home was silent, awkward. I was embarrassed and angry with my church. How could people who claimed to know Christ be so insensitive and miss the entire goal of the Christian life, which is to be like Jesus? Instead of offering grace and showing people like me and my friends a vision for what it means to follow Jesus, a bunch of Christians had gathered to make jokes at the expense of people like us?

I wondered how many of the men in that room struggled with their sexual orientation. I wondered how many of them had family members, close friends, neighbors, or coworkers who were somehow barred from the heteronormative dream that church often elevated. It seemed so disconnected, so uncaring.

SEEING CHRIST IN AN UNLIKELY FACE

But my own idol was about to be tested in no uncertain terms.

Because of my relationship with Thomas, I became increasingly passionate about finding biblical support for same-sex marriage. Ironically, just like the people I was so harshly critiquing, I was idolizing marriage. I wanted to marry someone like Thomas so I could have a holy and sexually pure relationship like my straight married peers. I wanted to belong.

Thomas had dark hair and green eyes. Our political views were worlds apart, but we could tease each other about controversial topics. The two of us drove around Sydney, enjoying the beaches and cafés. I often fell asleep in his arms as we sat in his car late into the evening. Thomas even came to my church a few times, though he preferred his Catholicism.

Our relationship grew. But I didn't understand why every time I was close to him, the Holy Spirit felt distant. I could just tell that something was off.

Finally, I made a commitment more than once of the kind that tend to be dangerous; God just might ask you to follow through on it. "God, please show me *directly* what you want for my life. I don't want to be influenced by church, by politics, or by anyone else's opinion. Whatever you show me, I'll obey it."

He did answer directly, but not through a vision or revelation. My relationship with Thomas continued to gnaw at me. A deeper voice told me that my sexual desires, no matter how sincere I was in my affection for another man, would never be the best for me.

It hurt so much. But gradually I realized that I needed to love Thomas the way Jesus loved him. And in order to love him like

Jesus did, I had to leave my relationship with him. What I wanted with Thomas could never be God's will for us.

I didn't want to face the reality that marriage might never be mine. It was so incredibly hard. But to follow Jesus, I had to let this dream die.

I remembered Jesus' words in Matthew 19:29: "Everyone who has left houses or brothers or sisters or father or mother or wife or children or fields for my sake will receive a hundred times as much and will inherit eternal life." I clung to the promise that he offered me *life*, not just brokenness and heartache. When I came to this realization and was ready to own it, I went to see Thomas. But I struggled to do what I knew was right.

We sat and talked. Sensing that I was dancing around an issue, he turned to me, serious. "David, what attracted me to you in the first place was your faith. You have a passion for God. It anchors you in a way I've never seen. I struggle to believe like you."

"Thank you, Tom," I said. "But I still think gay marriage is probably fine with God! It has to be!" Even I could hear the doubt in my voice, and I knew that I had just broached the concern at the center of all this.

He shook his head. "I'm getting in the way of your faith, David. I don't want to do that."

"No, Thomas. I love you," I said, holding back tears. This was too much. It just was. I couldn't follow through with the breakup.

In the following days, he picked me up and we drove back to his apartment to cheer me up and eat my favourite sushi. After the meal, we sat on the couch. I lay with my head on his chest, looking up at his stubble, and traced the shape of his chin with my finger. I lifted my head to kiss him.

"No, David. Stop." He pulled back.

"What's wrong?" I said.

He pushed me gently off his chest. "You're a Christian. I won't let you betray who you are. If I let you do this, you'll be devastated."

He was right. By staying with him, I was betraying my own conscience.

As I sat up and looked at Thomas that last time, I realized that in the very place I shouldn't have been searching for intimacy, I had found Jesus' love. Thomas put me and my identity as a Christian above his own desires. It was as if the Lord himself were gazing back at me through his eyes. I found the fulfillment of my desire for intimacy in its very denial.

That act of love from Thomas was a glimpse of the greater love I was searching for and would really satisfy me all along.

WHAT'S IN A MARRIAGE?

A year later the lesson of romantic idolatry I'd learned through my relationship with Thomas came back to me as my friend Tristan prepared for his wedding. We both ran a discipleship group and had seen the Lord do miraculous things, with many young men becoming Christians that year. We'd become close friends.

One night we realized together that it was Jesus who needed to be our first love, no matter what commitments or relationships might come our way, including Tristan's marriage. It was one of my first experiences of the incredible power of friendship to shape one's life and affections.

Finally, the couple's big day came. I sat in a pew and watched

Tristan's bride, Renée, enter the chapel and walk down the aisle. She reached her bridegroom, and her father blessed them as they joined hands. When Tristan and Renée exchanged vows and kissed, tears filled my eyes. I knew in this moment that marriage was something innate to God's own image and his intention for our humanity. He had made them male and female to reflect his glory. It was beautiful.

For the first time, I didn't feel the jealousy and loneliness I sometimes felt at weddings or when I was with my married friends. Instead I was filled with incredible joy that I could witness the love of Jesus Christ pictured in the bridegroom and his bride. The minister read from Song of Songs:

> Place me like a seal over your heart,
>   like a seal on your arm;
> for love is as strong as death,
>   its jealousy unyielding as the grave.
> It burns like blazing fire,
>   like a mighty flame.
> Many waters cannot quench love;
>   rivers cannot sweep it away.
>
> —*Song of Songs 8:6–7*

As I listened to these words, I realized that being gay did not exclude me from this kind of intense, faithful love. Like Tristan and Renée, I was part of the marriage between Jesus and his bride, the church, regardless of my sexual orientation. Marriage was that unique union in which, as Martin Luther said, "a man and wife united in the estate of matrimony are two in one flesh as God and man are united in the one person, Christ."[15] We weren't just celebrating their individual marriage; we were anticipating the future heavenly marriage of God and his people.

It was a fitting celebration for my new season ahead. Though I was sad to leave my church and friends like Tristan and Renée, I was excited to study abroad for a year. My dream had always been to return to France. It was my teenage romantic ideal, where I had wanted to walk in the footsteps of my intellectual heroes. I still hadn't forgotten my longtime dream of that handsome husband and our dreamy apartment in Paris.

Before I flew out, I poured my heart out to God. I sensed him saying, *David, I do not want to erase your dreams or delete your desires. I made you; I know you better than you know yourself. I know the ways you are broken, and I know the ways you will flourish. I gave you the desire to go back to France, and I am going to reinvent the dream that came from that desire all those years ago. Trust me, my son.*

There were lessons ahead to be learned, new dreams God wanted to give me. Was I ready to receive them?

CHAPTER 16

FACING FACTS IN FRANCE

Guide me in your truth and teach me, for you are God my Savior, and my hope is in you all day long.

—Psalm 25:5

Kosher grocers and delis lined the streets of the Jewish quarter of Strasbourg, France, where I'd moved into an antique Protestant chaplaincy building that also served as a student residence. My room, on the mid level of this grand building, was in the same building that was once home to renowned French theologian and philosopher Paul Ricoeur, whom I had studied in university classes years before. I noted that fact with a little thrill of satisfaction.

Just around the corner was the political science faculty, where I was completing the final year of my degree. Beyond that? A statue of the German poet Goethe, and only a little farther still, European Parliament.

It had been a long winter. Looking out my window, I watched the melting snow drip from the roofs. This was the first day it had been above freezing, and a white dusting still covered the city.

I longed for a thaw of my heart too. Without my Christian community in Australia, I was lonely. The European students I studied with seemed interested only in their future careers—administration and politics. I was interested in that too but longed for deeper connection.

I picked up an old journal and began reading it, remembering waypoints in my spiritual journey so far. One day, reading back in my journal, I recalled something a mentor in Sydney had told me: "Like a ship on the sea, God is going to give you a compass to navigate your way through Europe." I held on to those words.

The next week, I met another Christian at the political science faculty, and she introduced me to the Navigators student ministry. Its symbol, I discovered, was a sailing ship.

That was where I met my compass. Merrie, a Bible teacher who mentored Christian students, became my closest friend and confidant through our shared intellectual, political, and spiritual interests, and before I knew it, my heart was coming out of its freeze into a much warmer Strasbourg.

Every week I would arrive at her apartment building and ring the buzzer, eager for our time together. As the smell of fresh bread wafted up from the bakery downstairs, we talked about the gospel, philosophy, our encounters with God, the poor, and those in need. Merrie shared my love for food and cooked all kinds of French dishes during our visits. I'd never been loved so holistically by, or received this kind of hospitality from, an elder believer. Though she lived a frugal, God-dependent lifestyle and had known real poverty, she radiated warmth, wisdom, and a simple richness.

For more than thirty years, Merrie had dedicated her life to bringing the gospel to her beloved France, quietly making disciples among students and other people often left on the margins by the church. She even told me about a brief discussion in Rome her Christian friend had with none other than my onetime hero, Jean-Paul Sartre, shortly before he died. Sartre ended the conversation saying, "I'm not far from where you are with Jesus." Merrie's life inspired me.

I was also deeply encouraged by her strength and resolve as a celibate middle-aged woman. Three men had proposed marriage to her over the years, but each time she refused them because marriage did not align with her God-given calling. I filed this fact away. Such an example was new in my experience but remarkably compelling, as I felt the genuineness of being welcomed as family by this Christlike woman who'd chosen such a different life.

Merrie had an authority to speak into my life. She had truly given up everything for Jesus. She never judged me for my sexual orientation but embraced me as her own son. She told me she admired the way I had chosen to live, desiring to hear from God and follow his will. Through her example, she taught me to love and appreciate any church that believed in Jesus, from the small charismatic Lutheran church down the road to the mainline Protestant churches, as well as the conservative evangelicals, Pentecostals, and Roman Catholics who met in the cathedral.

I found in Merrie a marriage between the intellectual and existential sides of Christian faith. God knit a precious bond between us. This richer friendship, I started to see, came directly from Merrie's intimacy with Jesus. It seemed he had brought me to Strasbourg to meet her.

Months later, on Easter morning, the spires of the Strasbourg Cathedral pierced the purple sky as I walked down the *Rue des Freres* with Merrie, her hand resting on my arm. Soon the church bells announced it was midday, and people poured out of the cathedral after Mass. The city square was crammed with market stalls, and the restaurant terraces lining the streets were packed with holiday tourists enjoying traditional Alsatian food and sipping fine white wines.

As we browsed the busy market stalls, Merrie brought up the topic of homosexuality.

"David," she said gently, "you need to face the question of whether Jesus is Lord over all of your life, and the reality that same-sex desire will only lead you into sin."

I couldn't believe what I was hearing. If it had been anyone but Merrie, I would have snapped back a reply, but she had earned my trust.

"I'm not sure about that, Merrie," I stammered, flustered.

"David, I say this only because I really do love you. I know what it will cost you. But our lives are not about sex. Our lives are about serving Jesus and his kingdom."

I left the market early, upset by Merrie's words. Deep down, I knew there wasn't a hint of homophobia in them, just pure love, accompanied by truth. She understood what it would cost me to believe them—understood even in a way I couldn't, from decades of sacrifice. Real Christian discipleship, she had told me before, had to involve moments of tough love—it was costly.

Sure, she had my best interests in mind. But that didn't mean it didn't feel like an ocean of pain. *I just wish I could revise what God said in Scripture,* I thought as I walked home.

But her words haunted me, amplified by a whisper in my heart: *He wants all of your heart, all of your worship.*

I thought back to the weeks before I left Australia, when I was devouring everything I could read by Henri Nouwen.

His experience was so similar to my own. He was a same-sex-attracted Catholic priest who left his academic life at Princeton to join a community and care for mentally disabled people. Henri wrote of our never-ending struggle to overcome self-rejection and simply know that we are God's beloved children.

This divine love was what I desired more than anything, even romantic love. Almost all my past boyfriends had told me I was searching for something far greater than what they could offer me. For a little while, I'd dated a fashion writer, who, after a concert, broke off our relationship. "David," he said, hugging me goodbye, "you're too profound for me."

I struggled for weeks there in Strasbourg. One night I collapsed on my bed, exhausted by my internal dialogue. I was sick of struggling with my sexuality over three years of being a Christian.

I thought back, reviewing my life so far. All my life, I had believed that romantic love was what would make me whole. But it couldn't. Every relationship had only left me more vulnerable and in need of love.

Perhaps, I thought, *I can live like Merrie, right at the center of God's kingdom, to invite people deeper into God's love. Maybe the desire for a partner was a distraction from some greater task I've been given.*

Not long before, I would have greeted that idea with no uncertain language. But Merrie's love gave me the strength to really consider it.

CHAPTER 17

GOD'S GREATER ROMANCE

> God has bound everyone over to disobedience so that he may have mercy on them all. . . . Therefore, I urge you, brothers and sisters, in view of God's mercy, to offer your bodies as a living sacrifice, holy and pleasing to God—this is your true and proper worship.
>
> —*Romans 11:32; 12:1*

It was spring in Strasbourg, and I opened the large windows that overlooked the *Avenue de la Fôret Noire* and sat down at my reading desk. One of my favorite pastimes was watching people from this vantage point, and soon I recognized everyone in the neighborhood. That Saturday morning, the sun shone over the misty street. I watched an old man cross to the bakery to buy bread, and breathed deeply. This was *France.*

Reading was another of my favorite ways to spend free time. My too-small bookcase overflowed with secondhand novels, and I was currently working through a French translation of Hemingway. His sparse style made it easier to enjoy the story and decipher bits of the French language I hadn't mastered.

I had been shopping and bought fresh chicken Kiev to serve

my Swedish friends who were coming to study that evening. New friendships meant that the loneliness of the winter had abated, though I was romantically frustrated, watching so many of my friends pair off into relationships. France seemed like an impossible place to be alone. It was made to be shared.

My conversation with Merrie weeks before still bothered me. As I sat on my bed reading, I suddenly threw my book down. "God," I said out loud, "I need a direct answer from you. I can't keep living this way. Do I have a romantic future or not?"

Silence.

As I bustled about to get ready for my guests, I struggled with this. It bit at every part of my identity.

Two days before, I'd attended a book launch at Librairie Kleber, a large bookstore in town, for *Le Triangle Rose,* the memoir of Rudolf Brazda.[16] This stout and vivacious elderly man was the last living gay Holocaust survivor. He'd shared his incredible story of survival, and I couldn't get it out of my mind. One hundred thousand gay men and women had been persecuted by the Nazis, many of them exterminated. Brazda, the son of Czech immigrants to Germany, spent thirty-two months in the Buchenwald camp in central Germany before he was freed by American forces on April 11, 1945.[17] The title of his book referred to the pink triangle the Nazis made him wear, identifying him, alongside thousands of others, as homosexual.

Brazda had shown us his concentration camp tattoos and talked about being beaten by Nazi guards. Once he had three teeth knocked out and was told he was going to be executed. He survived only because two guards, one of whom had feelings for Brazda, helped by getting him off hard-labor quarry duty. The possibly gay guard also gave him stolen food rations. In late

March 1945, as the Allies closed in, another SS officer hid him in the camp's pig shed so he wouldn't be taken on a forced death march.[18]

"I lay there with the pigs for fourteen days until the Americans came," he said, reading from his book. "After that I was a free man. Others died, but I came through."[19]

I felt my soul wrestling with God as I listened to the atrocious things the Nazis did to Brazda. In a profound way, I was in awe of his strength through such horrendous evil and suffering. I had been a part of this community; in a different place and time, I too would have faced the death that looked him in the eye. As a Christian, did I have to deny the reality of my same-sex desires entirely? Was every aspect of my past—even with the strong and beautiful things about it—doomed to be erased and forgotten? As a Christian, did I have to ignore the history of LGBTQI people and the freedoms people like him had suffered so much to gain?

At one point, Brazda's eyes met mine. I felt a solidarity with him that, while different, felt something like the bond of fellowship I often felt when I first met Christians. I remembered that in the Beatitudes, Jesus says the poor in spirit are blessed, for theirs is the kingdom of God. Though Brazda and I had very different lives, there was a deep reciprocity of spirit—something like this poverty of spirit.

It was as if the harrowing dehumanization he suffered exposed a part of my felt alienation. I could no longer ignore the complexity of my soul and the life I was called to. I had deceived myself, thinking that it was easier just to run away from the reality of being SSA/gay, when actually God wanted to redeem and use it. A harder path was set calling for a true poverty of spirit.

Brazda's story gave me the courage to really face the conundrum of my faith and sexuality.

I hopped onto my bicycle and headed home, knowing I would never forget that day at Librairie Kleber. Something else was on my mind too. Many Christians had encouraged me to use the term same-sex attracted to distance myself from the gay world, but somehow this just didn't work when I spoke to people outside Christian circles. Others said, "Don't call yourself gay! You're making your sexuality your identity." Such a statement, while seemingly caring, dismissed the nuanced reality of my story. There was something in our shared reality of living with these desires and bodily differences that contained a shared history, a common experience. This aspect didn't have to conflict with my choice to follow Christ or what I chose to do with my homosexuality. While it risked confusing some Christians, no term was perfect and had limitations, but I knew God was calling me to be transparent about this part of my identity.

As I weaved through the streets, I asked, *God, what's your response? Do you want me to stop identifying myself as gay altogether?*

Jesus' broken body flashed before me. *I died with them,* his quiet voice said. *I entered into the evil of death and injustice.*

God, I realized, didn't dismiss the suffering of the gay community. Rather he identified with unjust human suffering on the cross. He said it mattered.

The Suffering Servant of Isaiah 53 knew what it was like to be led to death, just like many of those gay Holocaust survivors. As God's Son, his death was able to deliver others from sorrow, injustice, pain, and sin. That meant I needed to give him my pain, not hide parts of myself. While my homosexuality was secondary to Jesus' claim on my life, it still was important to him. It was part of my broken humanity, a humanity he took on himself in order to redeem it.

After meeting Brazda, I knew I could never forget or run away from the reality of my same-sex desires, even though I knew being gay or SSA could never be my ultimate identity. It would only ever be secondary to the lordship of Jesus. Yet I had to find a faithful way to live it out. I had no idea what that would mean, but I knew it started with honesty, not running away from this aspect of my current reality. I trusted that Jesus would lead me, just as he always had.

GIVING GOD MY HOMOSEXUALITY

One day, not long after the event at Librairie Kleber, I sat on my bed yet again. "God," I cried out loud once more, "I have a body. Where do you expect me to find the intimacy you created me for? I thought it was not good for man to be alone. Lord, I need an answer."

David, his quiet voice whispered, *my church is meant to be that body to you.*

"Really?" I was skeptical. "I haven't been able to find a church where that kind of intimacy is even possible. I need a partner."

What came next was as clear as it was odd. *I'm sending you a birthday present.*

My birthday was just a few days away. When the day came, I just about ran to check the mail. Sure enough, there was a small parcel from Joshua, my friend who'd invited me to hear Don Carson. Even though he had entirely forgotten about my birthday, his package just happened to arrive on it.

I tore it open. It was a book. "*Washed and Waiting*," I read, "by Wesley Hill." It was a reflection on homosexuality and Christian faithfulness.

Joshua had scrawled on a little note, "A friend recommended this, and I thought it would bless you."

I devoured the book, astonished by how closely Hill's story mirrored mine. Both joy and pain filled my heart as I read. He had resolved to call himself a celibate gay (or SSA) Christian. Even if Hill was raised as a Christian, unlike myself, I'd never heard of someone doing this before, but it fit so naturally with what I'd just experienced after hearing Brazda. Hill's words reflected my own theological intuitions and my identity as a Christian as well as the reality of being a man attracted to men. The way he put Jesus Christ at the center of his life inspired me.

Hours passed, and I flew through the pages. When I finally put the book down, a storm was brewing outside. I listened to the first water droplets hit the roof, accompanied by a dramatic thunderclap. I thought again of Paul's words in Romans 12: "I urge you, brothers and sisters, in view of God's mercy, to offer your bodies as a living sacrifice, holy and pleasing to God—this is your true and proper worship" (v. 1). And another verse from Paul, this one in 1 Corinthians 6: "All other sins a person commits are outside the body, but whoever sins sexually, sins against their own body" (v. 18).

I knew beyond doubt that God was asking me to do what I had never thought I could: give him my homosexuality and choose celibacy. It was that simple. It was also that hard.

From a sort of loving, desperate surrender, I prayed. "Lord," I whispered, "you died on the cross for me. You gave me your body. How could I not give you my body in return? How could

I hold back my sexuality, let alone my money, my plans, my affections, my whole self? Anything less wouldn't be true worship."

This was different from my other times of surrender. God had given me all of himself in his Son and Spirit, and it was time to give him all of myself. My gay identity had to bow to Jesus Christ, and that meant being willing to live without a partner for the remainder of my life.

His love called me to relinquish the desires warring against my repentance. I gave them over to him and was swept into his arms. This was the greater romance, the one true love that could fulfill me, far more than sex or any relationship could.

In that beautiful moment, I couldn't know that my heartfelt commitment to celibacy was about to clash with my long-held dream of finding romance in France.

CHAPTER 18

ROMANCE IN FRANCE

If you let this chance pass, eventually, your heart will become as dry and brittle as my skeleton. So, go get him, for Pete's sake!

—*The old artist "Glass Man" in* Amélie

This is what the LORD says: "Cursed is the one who trusts in man, who draws strength from mere flesh and whose heart turns away from the LORD."

—*Jeremiah 17:5*

Spring had ripened into a warm summer. I sat with Merrie and friends from church, watching Bastille Day fireworks light up the July sky. The crackling fireworks and the cheering crowd reached a crescendo, and the burst of colors became a kaleidoscopic blur. *Red. White. Blue.* As I stared at them, my mind drifted, until it settled on a now-familiar face. *Jerome.* It felt like I'd just met him. I couldn't stop thinking about him.

It all started a week after my decision to surrender my sexuality to God. I was in the library with a pile of books on my desk, nose down, working. I had looked up from the stack of reading, just for a moment, and my heartbeat quickened. There was a handsome student I hadn't seen before—French, I thought. He saw me looking and smiled back. I quickly ducked behind my books, trying to act as if nothing had happened. But something had.

I continued to read and study, but my furtive glances were noticed. My friend Margarite, a law student and the reigning socialite of the class, tapped me. "David," she whispered with a smile, "I saw you looking at Jerome."

"Huh?" I said, feigning ignorance. But my face betrayed me.

"Don't be *ridiculous*." She giggled. "Jerome came over to me a while ago. He likes you. I've set up a drink for you two tomorrow night. And you're *going*, by the way."

My heart pounded. My dream of a French romance was here. I calmed myself down and shook my head no, but before I knew it, she was over at Jerome's desk responding for me.

Jerome's dark brown eyes stared at me through broad-rimmed glasses. "Bonjour, David," he mouthed, and something in me melted.

How much could it hurt to meet and talk? We got together for drinks the following night, and over the next weeks, I found myself spending every other day with Jerome. He was charming and brilliant. We went to the cinema to watch art house films, dipped our croissants in coffee at cafés, and discussed European politics and his plans to work as a political journalist or public servant. I started to forget about celibacy. We were just friends, and then more than friends. I was falling in love.

One evening Jerome kissed me under a full moon near the Palais Universitaire. Its beautiful facade was decorated with statues of philosophers looking down on us—whether in approval or displeasure, I couldn't tell.

The battle line was drawn between my love for God and my love for Jerome. I knew I was called to love God more than I desired this romantic relationship. I knew it was not God's will for me. But right now, I simply didn't care.

"I love you, Lord, but this is my dream," I told him. "A boyfriend. A husband. A partner. A lover. A companion. Someone to share life with. You made me for this, and I want it. You allowed me to have same-sex desires, so you'll just have to deal with this. I never chose it; *you* did." I ignored my conscience and pursued a relationship, but I didn't shut God out.

One late Saturday evening, Jerome and I went to the cinema. It was empty except for us. After the film, we wound our way through the dark cobblestone streets, hand in hand, until the cathedral came into view. As bells announced it was midnight and we turned the final street corner, I knew Jerome was going to ask me up to his apartment.

That old French dream resurrected itself in front of me. *God, I know this is not your will, but I want this anyway,* I thought, looking briefly to heaven. *I want it more than you right now. I'm sorry.* We climbed the spiral stairs to the top floor. Outside his door, Jerome pulled me in for a kiss. His dark brown eyes stared back at me, and he smiled. Our foreheads touched for a moment. Our connection was palpable.

As we walked into the apartment, Jerome fixed me a quintessentially French *tisane,* or herbal tea. I joined him to drink it in his room. Sitting on the bed, we began to kiss.

Psalm 139:7–8 flickered through my mind, uninvited: *"Where can I go from your Spirit? Where can I flee from your presence? If I go up to the heavens, you are there; if I make my bed in the depths, you are there."*

David, do not try to give him the love only I can give him, God's voice whispered. *You are my son. Remember who you are.*

The war of loves grew intense. *God or Jerome.* My physical self was choosing Jerome over God, but my new heart knew it had to choose God over Jerome. I realized that my love for God was stronger than my desire for Jerome. This had never happened before! My heart, I saw, had been too touched by grace to accept broken sexual desires over worship of my beloved, Jesus.

I stopped kissing Jerome. "I can't do this," I said in French. "I'm a Christian."

"What do you mean?" he asked, puzzled. "I'm Catholic. There's nothing wrong with this. It's love. God *is* love. If you have issues," he said, smiling, "you can just go to confession." He tried to kiss me again.

"No, Jerome, I'm serious. I don't think you understand. Love isn't just a feeling. Love is Jesus Christ dying on the cross for us." I put my head in my hands, then looked up at him. "He is clear on homosexuality. His grace isn't a license to do what I want with my body."

His confusion melted into acceptance. Seeing my earnestness, he nodded. "I understand," he said, with the gentle intelligence I so appreciated in him.

I understood that I'd just made one of the hardest decisions of my life.

"On peut être des amis," I said, with tears in my eyes. "We can be friends."

At church that next evening, the pastor preached from 2 Samuel, focusing on the words of David: "I will not sacrifice to the Lord . . . an offering that costs me nothing" (24:24). God knew. That was it. God *knew.*

The choice to give myself completely to God was not one I made as an indifferent, unfeeling robot. My heart was tender, bleeding, human. And it was the costly sacrifice I was offering him, a sacrifice that cannot be put into words. It went against the natural forces that raged within me, but God promised me grace and resurrection strength to help in my weakness. I was becoming a real disciple.

And even as I lost something I so desired, I was given my life back, as Jesus promised, in return. It is difficult to describe the depths of intimacy I shared with Jesus Christ after that choice against Jerome as my lover. Jesus was there, as if he were in the room, even as I mourned what I had just lost.

Jesus understood my struggles and temptations: "Because he himself suffered when he was tempted, he is able to help those who are being tempted" (Heb. 2:18). He knew what total sacrifice looked like, since he had submitted all of himself to his Father to bring us the kingdom of God.

That scared me. It also opened a new horizon of possibilities, a new kingdom reality. I knew that the intimacy and love I now shared with God was worth suffering for. *This* was entering the fellowship of Jesus' sufferings (see Phil. 3:10).

Besides Merrie, not many believers had warned me about costly sacrifice in the Christian life. In my experience, the church barely talked about what Scripture said about being living sacrifices. Instead they settled for a comfortable, easy gospel, offering what Dietrich Bonhoeffer called "cheap grace." That meant there was no need to surrender our choice sins, our closely held dreams, our deepest desires that went against God's revealed will.

I longed, so deeply, for something more than that—his will, and not my own. And I had taken my first steps toward it.

FEARING GOD IS LOVING GOD

My year in Strasbourg ended, and I moved back to Sydney. Even while I missed my life in France, I was glad to be home in Australia.

After I returned, my questions about biblical interpretation resurfaced. I saw now (Don Carson's voice ringing in my mind) that much of my reading of Scripture had simply been interpreting it as saying what I *wanted* it to say—putting myself above the text. Besides studying the context and using reason as I read God's Word, there was also a relational aspect. I needed to have a healthy respect, a fear of the Lord. That relationship would put God's view above my own.

This fear isn't a cowardly, trembling thing. It doesn't come from fear of punishment or the understanding of God as cruel. It is simply the full acknowledgment that he is Lord, the only Lord, and we are not.

I read in Isaiah 11 that the Messiah was prophesied to have "the Spirit of the knowledge and fear of the Lord" (v. 2) and that he would "delight in the fear of the Lord" (v. 3). Jesus, this Messiah, I came to understand, perfectly modeled this awe and respect for God, and he offered and imparted it to me—to all Christians—through the power of the Holy Spirit. It was not something I could cultivate on my own, no matter how I tried.

This fear is a sign we are living in real, costly grace, not in cheap grace that requires no sacrifice and never allows God's Word to challenge or change us. Sadly, many Christians I observed seemed to live a lukewarm life that lacked this awe for God.

Søren Kierkegaard faced similar challenges from the nominal Christian culture and scholarship of his day. I resonated with his words: "The matter is quite simple. The Bible is very easy to understand. But we Christians are a bunch of scheming swindlers. We pretend to be unable to understand it because we know very well that the minute we understand, we are obliged to act accordingly. . . . Christian scholarship is the church's prodigious invention to defend itself against the Bible, to ensure that we can continue to be good Christians without the Bible coming too close."[20]

One Sunday at church, the preacher's message was on the fear of the Lord. He quoted Psalm 19, which says, "The fear of the Lord is clean" (v. 9 ESV), and talked about how "the commandment of the Lord is pure, enlightening the eyes" (v. 8 ESV). As he shared from Scripture, I was convicted of the uncleanness of my own heart. The two other churches I sometimes attended, I realized, did not fear God in this deeper way; that was the hesitation I'd felt there from the beginning! That was why the Spirit in me held back, even in the midst of some wonderful things they taught and did. The relationship with God was skewed. They simply didn't fear him in this clean, beautiful way. *If I don't have the fear of the Lord,* I thought, *my love isn't real.*

That night, I submitted my life anew to the lordship of Christ, yet another milepost on my road. I now knew I had to leave these other churches and commit to one for my heart to be clean. While that did not mean severing friendships with people I cared about, it did mean cutting the ties of official fellowship and attendance as a sign of my new commitment.

In subsequent weeks, many of the people from these churches harshly criticized my choice to be celibate. It was so hard. I loved these people! But I didn't turn back. The freedom I'd found was worth it.

PART 4

THE NEW IDENTITY

CHAPTER 19

UNDERSTANDING LOVE AND CELIBACY

Aim at Heaven and you get Earth thrown in. Aim at Earth and you get neither.

—C. S. Lewis

My people have committed two sins: They have forsaken me, the spring of living water, and have dug their own cisterns, broken cisterns that cannot hold water.

—Jeremiah 2:13

At this point in the book, you'll have to bear with me a bit as my story shifts. My journey to calling myself a celibate gay Christian is far from over (and will continue to develop through the final chapter), but publicly committing my life to celibacy as a gay Christian was a watershed moment. What I'd like to do now is begin to shift into more specifics about what I've learned (and am still learning!), to share the convictions and principles that inform that decision. My story is a testament to God's quiet revolution in my heart. But these principles, I pray, can be used as a manifesto for a revolution in *yours*.

During my time as an activist, we frequently used the famous slogan "Love is love" while fighting the orthodox Christian definition of marriage. Love, as we defined it, was our highest ideal and our sacred entity. That, in our minds, settled the issue.

But while our slogan was popular, it was shallow at best. "Love is love" doesn't mean that much semantically, and it provides no definition of what love actually is. Nor can it differentiate between the various *kinds* of human love and desire. Is it really all that simple? No! Love has many commonalities, but part of what makes the human experience so rich is the multiplicity of loves that we experience. A mother's love is not a friend's love. A friend's faithfulness and a total stranger's act of compassion are both touching and wonderful. But they are not the same—cannot be, should not be.

Love, I have come to learn, is not God. Flip that. God *is* love. The God revealed in Jesus Christ is the definition of love. This difference changes everything. We are caught up in arms greater than our own, feeling the possibility of being accepted not by our mirror but *by our maker*.

The cross is where that strange and holy God most clearly reveals his love. There he gave his very self so that the whole world could know him and enjoy the intimacy we were designed for, and without which everything else breaks down. Human romance and attempts at religion can never provide lasting meaning. Only God can. In that sense, the cross is God's intimate act of self-giving, his gentle way of critiquing our love of money, sex, self, romance, fame, and, above all, power. These weaker loves, these idols we raise in our own image, could never compare with his infinitely greater love.

Jesus taught that both the worst sin and the most sacred worship originate from the same place: the heart. Think of that revolutionary concept! What does it mean? Simply, that God's love should displace all others and occupy the primary space in our hearts. It is, simply, what we were made for.

As Christians, the romance we should most celebrate is the marriage of heaven and earth, between Christ, the Bridegroom, and his bride, the church. It is the greatest of all love stories.

But notice this: the faithfulness of intentional celibacy is part of this love story. Both Christ and the bride ought to have only one lover. Practically, all lesser human loves, even the incredible intimacy of marriage, is a half shadow of that great love we were made to experience.

Let me be clear: this does *not* mean that we are all called to celibacy or that it makes one a super-Christian. That can turn to idolatry of lifestyle as much as marriage. But the core *skills* of celibacy—discipline, self-control, choosing a greater love at the sacrifice of a lesser—these are all key Christian skills pointing straight to the heart of Christ. No matter your calling, single or married, you must grow in them to grow in Jesus.

So why do most Christians seem far more concerned with romantic love than with God's great story? In many congregations, when an engagement or wedding is announced, there is often greater enthusiasm than when God is worshiped. In contrast, when someone commits themselves to celibacy, there is no celebration. The person is regarded as an abnormality.

Yes, biblical marriage is a beautiful expression of romantic love that glorifies God. But as Wesley Hill says, "The New Testament views the church—rather than marriage—as the primary place where human love is best expressed and experienced."[21] For C. S.

Lewis, it was not the loves in and of themselves that were bad, whether romantic or family love, but the *order* in which they were placed in the human heart.[22] It sounds like heresy in our culture, but romantic and sexual love are not the deepest expressions of our humanness. Unconditional love—God's love—is.

In his essay *Deus Caritas Est,* Pope Benedict XVI distinguishes between *agape,* that perfect, self-sacrificial love of God, and *eros,* that passion of sexual yearning, love, or desire for life and union most of us are so familiar with. *Agape* love, he wrote, sanctifies and transforms eros by turning it toward the worship of God—rechannelling our passions to further his kingdom.

And Pope Benedict XVI is not alone! On the other side of the cultural room, the gay Catholic writer and activist Andrew Sullivan wrote that he believes "we live in a world . . . in which respect and support for *eros* has acquired the hallmarks of a cult." In his book *Love Undetectable,* he states,

> The great modern enemy of friendship has turned out to be love. By love, I don't mean the principle of giving and mutual regard that lies at the heart of friendship [but] love in the banal, ubiquitous, compelling, and resilient modern meaning of love: the romantic love that obliterates all other goods, the love to which every life must apparently lead, the love that is consummated in sex and celebrated in every particle of our popular culture, the love that is institutionalized in marriage and instilled as a primary and ultimate good in every Western child. I mean *eros,* which is more than sex but is bound up with sex. I mean the longing for union with another being, the sense that such a union resolves the essential quandary of human existence,

> the belief that only such a union can abate the loneliness that seems to come with being human, and deter the march of time that threatens to trivialize our very existence.[23]

Those who define themselves through *eros* are actually seeking the transcendence of union with God. But they will never find it in human relationships. Looking there, they set themselves up for the heartbreak of a lifetime. We humans are caught in a love triangle of our own, for there are relationships between *agape* and *eros,* without doubt. But we have to choose *agape*—getting *eros* thrown in, to paraphrase Lewis.

As I look at our messy humanity, my heart breaks for God. We choose against him, nearly constantly. He is our jilted divine lover. He designed the good things of marriage and sexuality to be a means to worship him, not the object of our worship. But as the apostle Paul explains in Romans 1, we have all committed idolatry by exchanging the Creator for created things.

THE SACRED GIFT OF CELIBACY

Often when Christians focus on the world's sins, we neglect to communicate the solution: the love of Jesus Christ. In failing that way, we condemn people before they've even had the chance to know God's grace and understand that he is what they are really seeking.

Hear me well: homosexuality is not an evangelistic issue. It is a discipleship issue. So we must approach it that way. But we also need to remember that without a knowledge of God's grace, the gift of the Spirit, and an understanding of God's satisfying love, discipleship kills rather than gives life, condemns rather than convicts. Celibacy is no different. Gay or same-sex-attracted celibacy must be a response to God's love, not a legalistic bottling up of our human desires. It is about the redirected affections of a transformed heart.

Once we belong to Christ, we all—no matter our orientation—need to be discipled by him in the Spirit and be willing to be purified in our desires. Churches must not leave LGBTQI people in the dark pastorally and theologically about their particular situation. If they do, the entire body suffers from the idolatrous effects of a disordered love in the whole church body.

Over the years since my conversion, I have seen many initiatives, such as Matthew Vines' Reformation Project, which promote the affirmation of same-sex marriage in the church. Matthew Vines writes, "Christians throughout history have affirmed that lifelong celibacy is a spiritual gift and calling, not a path that should be forced upon someone."[24]

I agree that we must be careful not to present celibacy as a moral code. But what many biblical revisionists overlook is that *both* celibacy and marriage are a calling to find our fulfillment in Christ. Celibacy is neither an easy gift nor a repressive burden. It is an opportunity—an opportunity, not that different from marriage, to trust in God's capacity to provide for our need for intimacy. *Forsaking all others* . . . Do the words of the marriage vow ring hollow when we speak them to God? Any lack we presently experience in celibacy can be supplied with what Nouwen describes as the three qualities of God's love in us: intimacy (closeness), fecundity (fullness), and ecstasy (self-sharing). The poverty of spirit experienced in celibacy provides the opportunity for a deeper experience of divine love.[25] This is not to dismiss the real sacrifices of the celibate life. (Trust me, I know them.) But it gives them their proper context.

In Isaiah 56, the prophet receives a word from God about the future acceptance of eunuchs, or people whose sexual orientation or gendered state is different from the norm. The fulfillment of this prophetic text was God's embrace of the Ethiopian eunuch in Acts 8 after Jesus' resurrection. This story was radical in a society that saw eunuchs, or sexually-other people, as unclean and unable to enter God's holy presence in the temple.[26] But today, because of Jesus, LGBTQI people are welcomed into the church, the family and temple of God.

The apostle Paul, like many of the Christians after him, was also celibate in a society that expected marriage. In other places in the New Testament, the celibate life is seen as godly and a sign of dedication to Jesus. Revelation 14:4 says those who decide to remain celibate are the firstfruits of Christ's saving work: "[Those who remained celibate] follow the Lamb wherever he goes. They were purchased from among mankind and offered as firstfruits to God and the Lamb." It echoes Isaiah 56, which promises eunuchs "a name better than [having] sons and daughters" (v. 5)—the very name of Jesus Christ, who was himself single and childless. If Jesus was celibate and the ultimate example of human flourishing for all of us, gay or straight, then isn't it clear that celibacy is not an inhumane sentence for gay people like me but actually a legitimate, and even honorable, choice?

The church needs to return to a view of celibacy as a valid option and a sacred gift to give in response to Jesus' love. If the church does not recognize and value this truth, the lives of celibate gay Christians will be indescribably difficult, and the church will remain locked in idolatry.

In Christ, I discovered, my romantic status no longer defines my value, my wholeness, or my well-being. The gospel has become increasingly good news to me because in my celibacy, I am promised a name of precious worth. Much like the apostle Paul, who considered himself a spiritual father to Timothy and Titus, as a celibate gay man, I can sire spiritual children through the gospel.

Embraced, fulfilled, loved. I was learning that I am all of this and more, and I was eager to see how Christ would use me next to further his kingdom.

CHAPTER 20

BIBLE COLLEGE AND MOVING TO OXFORD

He guides me along the right paths for his name's sake.

—*Psalm 23:3*

Delight yourself in the LORD, and he will give you the desires of your heart.

—*Psalm 37:4*

The end of my undergraduate education had come, all too quickly. I had to decide what to do next. While I saw all of my life as worship to Jesus Christ, I wanted to spend concentrated time seeking God's presence and person. So at my church's New Year's service, a time to consecrate the year ahead to God, I responded by committing to attend a one-year course at Bible college. This was, for me, a Psalm 23 moment. *Father,* I prayed, *lead me to graze on green pastures, to be by still waters, and to spend my time in your house.*

Taking a year off from pursuing a career was an expression of love for Jesus. At the time, I had doubts about how such a school could really address my deeper needs, so choosing to go was an act of deep trust. But I wanted to mature in my relationship with him.

The decision to die to my sexuality had changed me. Strangely, I was even becoming *grateful* for my struggles. They had pointed me to God. That much was undeniable.

I still had unanswered questions. Lots of them. But I knew God's presence was with me every day. The relationship just required patience. He would not necessarily tie up every loose end or answer every question. But the faith was there. I'd seen him work. He'd work again.

In hindsight, that year at a small Bible college was the best year of my life in terms of growing closer to him. I heard his voice clearly, encountered him powerfully. One particular class had a profound impact on me. The teacher suffered from an acute respiratory disease that caused a spluttering cough between his words. It was a poignant reminder of our mortality, that our bodies, our desires, and this world are not as God ultimately intends. Between the professor's coughs, I received words of life.

REDEEMING THE PAST

One day, after that year ended, I slid into my car and headed to a job interview at a Christian aid organization. Turning up my favorite worship song, I praised God for making me right with him through Jesus, lifting the pressure of death and sin from my shoulders.

As I drove, I reflected that I was convinced like never before that "neither death nor life, neither angels nor demons, neither the present nor the future, nor any powers, neither height nor depth, nor anything else in all creation, will be able to separate us from the love of God that is in Christ Jesus our Lord" (Rom. 8:38–39).

I walked into the small, open office, nervous and excited for my interview. If I got the job, perhaps my inner activist could finally find an outlet through helping communities in developing nations.

I recognized a few people, familiar faces from Christian events I'd been involved in. One stood out in particular. I stared a little. He didn't see me. *Where do I know him from?* The subconscious confusion lasted only a split second. It was Michael. Wait, *Michael?*

Michael. My friend from that fateful love triangle at university five years ago. I couldn't believe it. Last I knew, he was an atheist. He really *disliked* Christians. What were the chances he'd be here, on the other side of Sydney, working for a Christian organization? Yet here he was. I felt like I'd been punched in the gut. I was so ashamed to see him after what had happened between me and Samuel, his ex-boyfriend.

I turned quickly, rushing to the bathroom area to remain out of view. Needing confirmation, I pointed over to his desk. "Who's that?" I asked a staffer nearby. She smiled. "That's Michael. He volunteers here." Afraid of being spotted, I ducked into the bathroom. *God, what's going on? Why is Michael here? What are you trying to say?*

I heard Jesus' voice respond to me: *You are justified by my death and resurrection for you. Do you really believe it? Do you really believe my blood was enough?*

I'm not sure I really do. I was shocked at my response.

I've freed you from the past, he told me. *You are no longer condemned. You are a different person, my new creation. Don't be ashamed. Walk back out there.*

I took a deep breath and walked out.

I got the job. As the weeks passed, I was asked to become Michael's overseer. I knew we needed to talk. I had so many questions, and something vital to say to him.

At first he didn't want to meet me for lunch outside of work. I couldn't really blame him, but we needed a private space to talk. Finally, he agreed.

Sitting across from him, I said, "Michael, I know this may seem crazy to you, but I am an entirely different person from who I was five years ago. I've been saved and transformed by Jesus Christ. I live a very different life." I looked down, then back at him. "I just want to say how sorry I am for what happened with Samuel. I was in the wrong. Will you forgive me?"

He put down his coffee. "I'm sure you're convinced of all that, David, but that simply won't do."

Michael didn't openly forgive me. But somehow I left that meal with a closure I never thought I would have. Driving home, I heard Jesus say, *David, I didn't just die for your sins. I also died to transform the* consequences *of your sins.*

Over our final months of working together, Michael's attitude toward me changed. While still avowedly agnostic, one day at a prayer meeting, he revealed that he had contracted a serious disease and his father had been diagnosed with cancer. Our community was able to be there for him. I was grateful for the opportunity to apologize to him personally, and, in the limited way that our strained relationship allowed, to be a friend in his time of need. There was not full restoration. But there was a new kind of equilibrium. A peace.

Is this not the unique power of the Christian gospel? For all the remaining messiness, for all the rough edges that result from the consequences of our actions, can anything else reconcile and restore the most broken situations and people? Oh, the hope for all of us! It is profound.

BECOMING AN APOLOGIST

The Sunday after that job interview, I met my friends from Bible college at church. After the sermon, a team of ministry leaders invited people to come up for prayer. When I stepped forward, an Armenian man named Leon, whom I knew only from afar, said the oddest thing: "David, God is showing me you will study in beautiful old libraries, poring over old books, with a Bible open at the center of it all. God has called you to study, speak, and write for him."

I hadn't told anyone (except my parents) that weeks before, at the suggestion of a mentor and friend, I had applied for a course in theology at the University of Oxford. I took this message from Leon as confirmation from God that Oxford would happen.

And sure enough, it did. Six months later I had left my job at the aid organization, crossed the world, and found myself back in the beautiful streets of Oxford, preparing to study theology. As a student concurrently at the Oxford Centre for Christian Apologetics and the University of Oxford, I hoped to grow as a writer, speaker, and communicator. I was to be trained in apologetics and evangelism by greats like John Lennox and Michael Ramsden, and I was given access to those old libraries Leon had mentioned. *This is surreal,* I thought. It felt like a dream.

As I walked down the long streets from my college, I could not believe I was here. I had been admitted to one of the world's great universities. The sound of church bells and the sight of blooming flowers covering the lawns filled me with joy, and the old buildings reminded me of one of my favorite poets, Gerard Manley Hopkins. Everywhere I looked in this city, God was speaking his love tenderly to me.

I walked past the Martyrs' Cross outside Balliol College, commemorating where the English Reformers Latimer and Cranmer were burnt at the stake for their beliefs. Before his death, Latimer wrote, "We shall this day light such a candle, by God's grace, in England, as I trust shall never be put out." There was something about their sacrifice that filled me with hope. Despite the daily struggle I still faced over my sexuality, I knew that like these men, I was willing to die for my faith. We were connected by the same Spirit.

All around the university, rainbow flags flapped in the wind. Their presence both troubled and pleased me—a reminder of still feeling in-between. Were they a sign of my liberty or of my oppression? I didn't fit in the gay world anymore, and I didn't fully fit in the Christian one either.

I turned my eyes back to the mosaic of the Martyrs' Cross on the asphalt. *We will all die,* I thought. *But the question is, what we will die for?* Like the martyrs who died on that ground, I had to be willing to give my whole life to following Christ, even if that meant living a deeply unpopular life and being mocked or disdained.

I continued my walk past Blackwell's bookstore, where Daniel, my mother's colleague, had bought me Richard Dawkins's *The Selfish Gene* ten years before. As I selected books for that term's classes, I purchased John Lennox's *Gunning for God,* his response to Dawkins's New Atheism. *What a difference these years made,* I thought.

I made my way through the backstreets and past the old sights: the Bodleian Library, Sheldonian Theatre, and Radcliffe Camera. After walking through High Street and past Merton College, I entered the old gate of Christ Church Meadow. As I stood looking at the football pitch surrounded by budding daffodils and crocuses, I pictured my fifteen-year-old self standing just yards away and remembered my words of self-doubt: *I'm not good enough. I'll never study here.*

Yet here I was.

God had lifted up, loved, and saved that self-doubting gay boy. He had brought him, through the most unlikely of events, back here. A decade before, I was one of the last people in the world who'd be training as a Christian apologist. But now I stood with a bag full of books and a heart full of love for Jesus.

Under those impossible spires, God the Father was giving me, his son, the desires of my heart.

CHAPTER 21

DRAWING THE LINE: ACCEPTANCE VERSUS AFFIRMATION

Without knowledge of self, there is no knowledge of God. Our wisdom, insofar as it ought to be deemed true and solid wisdom, consists almost entirely of two parts: the knowledge of God and of ourselves. But as these are connected by many ties, it is not easy to determine which of the two precedes and gives birth to the other.

—John Calvin

The heart has its reasons of which reason knows nothing.

—Blaise Pascal

I was working in Oxford one evening when a ding on my laptop announced I'd received an email. To my shock, I saw it was from the Archbishop of Canterbury's office, inviting me to speak at the Church of England's General Synod about my journey with homosexuality.

Around that same time, a flurry of voices—from within the Church of England and also from the wider evangelical world, including Tony Campolo and Jen Hatmaker—had made pronouncements in support of gay relationships. Just that week, I had been dealing with deep discouragement after hearing that someone prominent in the celibate gay Christian world came out in support of same-sex relationships and marriages in the church. It was a struggle to stand with God, hold to what I knew his Word taught, and not succumb to the immense pressure to affirm such unions.

Others in the church, afraid of repercussions or being judged from the sidelines, kept their mouths shut. It all took a toll on celibate gay Christians like me. It felt as if our personal call to faithfulness and sacrifice to God were insignificant, ignorant, or not based on serious convictions.

Other than in certain corners of the church, and in groups like Spiritual Friendship and Living Out, I had not seen an orthodox perspective that took seriously both the reality of same-sex desire and the biblical witness. People seemed to choose one or the other.

Perhaps pain had blinded us, not only to the Bible but to our own honest hearts. We needed a nuanced approach that acknowledged and accepted our fallen desires but did not affirm their practice, instead using them to invite us into deeper relationship with Christ and the church. We needed a revolution of leadership, beginning with our hearts.

I said yes to the archbishop's invitation, which one ought to do in such situations.

As I prepared to address the synod, I thought about how Alan Manning Chambers had closed Exodus International, which transitioned from an ex-gay therapy ministry in the eighties to a parachurch ministry to provide pastoral support for same-sex-attracted Christians. Most of those involved in Exodus in its last days repudiated the pseudo-Freudian therapies it once promoted. Following an evolution in its understanding of homosexuality, the mainstream ex-gay movement took its last breath.

When Chambers closed the ministry, he said it was the responsibility of the church, not a parachurch ministry, to support same-sex-attracted or gay Christians. Although in many ways I was happy about Exodus's closure, I also saw there was little place in the church for people like me. We desperately needed voices to speak up and offer wisdom and guidance to churches seeking to reach out to same-sex-attracted individuals.

The synod was to meet in York. The date came, and I rode the train north. When I arrived, I felt a heavy responsibility to be prophetically clear as I shared my testimony. I was speaking as a representative of Living Out, a UK-based organization for same-sex-attracted Christians. Three other younger panelists and I who were speaking at Shared Conversations, a closed event at the synod, were each given seven minutes to share our experience of being LGBTQI Christians.

I was the only panel member who believed the traditional biblical position that same-sex acts are sinful. I was the only one who mentioned our society's obsession with marriage and its idolatry of romantic love. The others shared mainly about the depth of their legitimate hurt and pain, but I did not hear any positive moral vision, nor was there any grappling with God's Word or with two thousand years of church tradition.

"What truly matters," I said, after sharing my story of finding Jesus Christ, "is not our view as the church or as a society. What matters is what *Jesus Christ* is saying to us. The lie we're telling ourselves is that compromising holiness will ensure church growth. That's false. Embracing and raising up those who are sexually faithful and obedient, as witnesses to our culture, *will* attract the world. Without holiness, Jesus Christ can't be seen in us by the world; and without love, the world will resist the truth of this holiness."

After I spoke, I thought about how in the Victorian era the tendency was to understand the body and its desires as essentially bad, but in today's society all the body's desires are perceived as good and infallible without filter. In response, the church risks falling into one of two extremes. In the first, we push back against that ideology and denigrate the body. The entire physical creation is seen as terribly bad, and hence we must escape the body and its desires in order to find holiness. In the second, we follow the world's lead and render the body supreme. The physical creation and our desires are seen as unquestionably good, meaning there is no fall and no sin.

Both extremes are anti-Christian. We risk either demonizing or elevating complex desires, which cannot fit neatly into straightforward categories of "sinful" or "acceptable." By necessity, the issue of gay marriage requires a complex response.

Having been in many relationships myself, I don't see gay romantic relationships as a separate sphere cut off from the kingdom, as something God is not at all involved with. There may be aspects of gay relationships or unions that Christians should learn to accept and recognize, such as the bond of friendship and the self-sacrificial love I have seen in many of my friends' unions. Christianity has room for affirming so much of the good and beautiful there, while still keeping traditional views of sexual expression and love.

For those in gay relationships or marriages who bravely

repent of sexual sin, the solution is anything but simple. It takes time, and many answers are going to be messy. Gay couples often have children and become a family unit. What is their call? Easy answers break down very quickly without the Spirit's leading and discernment.

What a gay person really needs—as does every one of us—is to embrace a new, God-given identity. We have been crucified with Christ, and it is no longer we who live but Christ who lives in us (Gal. 2:20). By definition, this new identity cannot live the old way. We need to repent and put away the old identity. In a gay person's case, the old identity is defined by same-sex desire. While celibacy and identifying as gay are in some sense compatible, staying in a sexually active relationship cannot be compatible with fully embracing a Christian identity. God's Word reveals that we are called to die to our sinful nature and to pursue holiness, by the power of the Spirit.

Every Christian, gay or straight, must offer their body as a living sacrifice to God, like Jesus did on the cross. This is, as Paul says, our spiritual act of worship (Rom. 12:1). That means that for both a gay person and a heterosexual person, living in a sex-obsessed culture, the crucifixion of our old nature and the embrace of our new one is the highest act of worship. This is where in denying ourselves, we receive a new self from God.

The question we must ask is not whether a gay relationship can be made holy. Rather the question is, do sexually active gay relationships reflect God's image, glory, will, and purpose? What matters is God's perspective, not our projection of what we want God to be like and to accept.

This discussion of sexual ethics is one for inside the church, and I do not wish to extend it into the state or political arena.

The church is called to live differently than the world. Its primary authority in all matters of faith, practice, and discipleship is Jesus Christ and the Scriptures that testify of him. Love and the purpose for our desires are defined by God, and no longer by us.

SAME-SEX DEBATE IN THE CHURCH

In Christianity, we generally see polarizing approaches to the question of same-sex marriage. Are gay relationships distinct from a marriage between a man and a woman? Some strongly say no; others vehemently say yes. There are others still who prefer not to say what they really think, to avoid consequences.

Activism has not helped, by hindering open discussion in both the church and society. This contributes to leaders who avoid making any comments, for fear of media abuse. The endless polarization makes celibate gay Christians feel like they have to pick a side, instead of focusing their attention on following Christ.

What does this debate look like, and what does each side's view of human nature have to do with it? Progressives claim that Christians who reject same-sex marriage are denying the equality, human rights, and innate dignity of LGBTQI people. They assume our internal desires are right because they are innate to our nature. Many progressives, although not all, label churches that hold to a traditional view of marriage as non-affirming, instantly discouraging onlookers by using a negative term.[27]

Progressives adopt the claim of Western culture, which says, "Whatever I desire is what I ought to have." But this view overlooks the fact that Jesus Christ alone can give meaning to our fallen nature and provide clarity for our desires. We see this with

Paul, who in his writings defines marriage and sexual vocation through Christ.[28] God is the one who shows us who we were created to be and who we are to become in him.

Those with the traditional view, on the other hand, maintain that same-sex marriage and sex acts are not permissible. When charitably understood, the traditional or orthodox view has nothing to do with homophobia or denying the equality or rights of LGBTQI people; it is simply a different vision of human sexuality and its purpose in marriage. It comes from a richness of belief, not a poverty of perspective. It's just not as simple as affirming or non-affirming.

I often find there is a progressive bias against celibate gay Christians like me. Some say we can't call ourselves gay unless we affirm same-sex expression. Ironically, this is similar to how some churches have treated and excluded gay couples. There is no real excuse for it, although I believe the progressive view is often driven by a fear of condemnation and an avoidance of real discipleship. Pain can block any of us from understanding obedience by grace and comprehending how a call to celibacy can be joyful, even life-giving. I'm not a traitor to the gay community. I'm just a celibate gay Christian. Is there room for me? Is there a stripe on the flag with my color on it?

What would it mean for both sides to come to a deeper biblical understanding? For those on the traditional end, it might mean being willing to live and love radically for Jesus. This would mean giving up false and empty religion that resists the real Jesus Christ; it would also mean rejecting the idols of wealth and family, being willing to see and respond to the needs of others, and giving up convenience and comfort for the sake of following Jesus.

For progressives, it could mean giving up the idols of sexual liberty, rejecting a victimhood or entitlement mentality, no longer shutting down those who disagree, and repenting of the pride that says, "I don't need the living God; I'll just appeal to my inner self."

Ultimately, both sides of this debate need to look to the resurrection, when one day there will be no same-sex *or* opposite-sex desire entirely analogous to what we now experience. In Matthew 22:29–30, Jesus said this to the Pharisees and Sadducees who asked him about divorce and marriage: "You are in error because you do not know the Scriptures or the power of God. At the resurrection people will neither marry nor be given in marriage; they will be like the angels in heaven." Like those he was speaking to, we are obsessed with marriage and romance. But these things are only a reflection of greater eternal realities! We are going to be transformed into so much more than sexual beings. Our very nature will be resurrected.

In the end, there will be no "right side" of this issue to be on. There will be only one side, the kingdom of Jesus Christ, and the incredibly rich and diverse people who fill it. It will be free from arguing, division, and the idolatry of self, and filled with resurrected people whose very natures are like Christ's.

I long for that day, pray for that day. I'm working for that day. But I wonder, can I start living it right now? Do I really have to wait?

CHAPTER 22

BELOVED FRIENDSHIP

One of them, the disciple whom Jesus loved, was reclining next to him.

—*John 13:23*

But love is lost; the way of friendship is gone, though David had his Jonathan, Christ his John.

—*George Herbert*

Chastity does not mean abstention from sexual wrong; it means something flaming, like Joan of Arc.

—*G. K. Chesterton*

On an early summer's day, I took a walk with my friend Mark. We went through a park, the setting where C. S. Lewis, W. H. Auden, and other literary figures had sat to write. It was our favorite spot to relax during the stressful term.

Our friendship had begun months earlier, when many others at Oxford were struggling to understand who I was and what my position on sexuality represented. Mark had admired my faith and decided he was going to make a concerted effort to get to know me.

He was from a small American town and had been a college football player. You couldn't find two people from such different backgrounds, yet we became great friends. Our lives were being radically transformed, and I loved seeing Christ at work in him.

We often attributed our easy closeness to the fact that he had a twin brother, so sharing deeper affection with other men came naturally to him. What had started as his choice to get to know me grew into the deepest Christ-centered male friendship I'd ever known.

We sat on the lawn near River Cherwell, chatting about our futures, then started laughing as we impersonated the idiosyncrasies of our eccentric professors. The whole park was filled with birdcalls, everything at its highest point of life. Dandelion spurs floated on the air, and the underleaves of the trees were the lush, intense green that only the heart of England seems to have perfected. Summer in Oxford was *special.*

As we sat in the grass, Mark reclined his head against me. I didn't have a modern category for this kind of closeness and almost flinched. Thoughts raced through my mind. *Isn't this gay?* I wasn't used to platonic male affection. One part of me, the optimistic part, loved it and enjoyed the freedom of friendship I had with Mark. Christ's presence seemed evident in the bond we shared. But another part of me, the realist, was worried.

I was unsure that this was even possible, considering my attractions to men. I truly sensed no lust, no possessiveness, either in me or in Mark. But somehow this demonstration didn't fit neatly into the category of brotherly love either. All the labels I'd been taught couldn't help me make sense of it.

I thought of the apostle John, who had reclined against Jesus at the table. There was room in that culture, in that relationship.

Had I found a friendship like that, in which such affection could be expressed without being sexualized? Perhaps this was how God had intended friendships all along. If so, was it a taste of the kind of friendship we will have in the heavenly future? If celibacy was indeed an invitation into this kind of relationship, it was surely good news for me.

While I didn't find Mark attractive (yet), he was male, and that spelled fear for me. I was afraid of losing this level of intimacy or having it become something else. If he married, friendships would naturally take a back seat for him. As a straight man, he had the option of finding a spouse. I did not.

Something changed the moment we touched like that. Things grew awkward, and our conversation on the lawn faded away. As we walked home, we didn't speak. Perhaps Mark too was unsure what to make of this level of friendship. Something undefined had arisen between us.

In the following weeks, he pulled back. We stopped walking or studying together. He started spending time with other friends.

WRESTLING WITH GOD

A few days later, as I sat at my favorite café, typing up a theology essay, I realized I was angry with God. I had thought I was free from that old voice of accusation, so different from the voice of his Spirit, that said, *You'll never be loved or accepted; you're nothing but a sexual and relational failure.* But here it was again.

I thought back to all those times I'd been let down, whether in friendships or romantic relationships. I realized that what I was really searching for was a safe, deep, and mutually respectful friendship. I needed a human to help embody God's love for me. It wasn't Mark's lying back against me that was significant; it was the *trust* that he, as a straight man, had shown me by doing so. He had communicated safety, acceptance.

I had finally experienced a deep bond with another man that wasn't, as far as I could tell, about sex or lust. *God, why would you let me experience such love for a friend and then take it away?*

I took a break from typing and sat thinking about how the love of Christian disciples should break any earthly categories we have for love. This love comes from another source, from above. It is the love that Jesus came to teach and model, a love that gives up its life for a friend.

The problem was that while I was—or at least thought I was—entirely comfortable with God because he is perfect, faithful, and never fails me, even through suffering, the love of other human beings terrified me. People, including me, are fickle, flaky, selfish. I didn't want to love my neighbors because I didn't trust their capacity to love me back. This reality stunned me.

Your life and ministry are worthless without these kingdom friendships, I felt God whisper to me. *I am not going to take away your desire for relationship with others.*

Still, I said to God, *I'm so angry that you won't take this desire for deep friendship with Mark away.*

From my studies, especially reading *Washed and Waiting,* it seemed that the Christian tradition had lost vision for this kind of relationship. We'd lost our categories for beloved communion outside of a sexual relationship. Was a love like the love David and Jonathan shared, a bond that was greater than romantic love, even possible? It seemed so removed from the broken masculinity I had seen.

I thought about how Jonathan's father, King Saul, hated his spiritual friendship with David and tried to kill Jonathan because of it (1 Sam. 20:33). In some sense, Jonathan was a type of Jesus, willing to give up his life for his friend. This biblical love seemed to have been entirely forgotten in our sex-obsessed society. Even the church rarely talked about it.

The story of Jesus and John had also always piqued my interest, and I was intrigued that according to tradition, John called himself the Beloved Disciple in his gospel. What a way to describe yourself! And yet it dawned on me that John took that title because he really understood how much Jesus loved him and how unique their friendship was. Calling himself the Beloved Disciple had nothing to do with pride but everything to do with the kind of relationship John experienced with Jesus.

John was at the cross with Jesus. He was the only disciple who remained faithful and stayed with Jesus as he suffered. Their bond pointed to a future reality—a love that every Christian would know with God and, one day, with every other Christian in eternity.

Imagine a world where all people shared this self-sacrificial love with God and each other! God's kingdom was infiltrating this present world, and it wanted to invade through the simple love of friends.

I sensed that God was teaching me one of the secrets of his kingdom: *David, you cannot bring the kingdom of heaven to earth until you've tasted heaven.* I was reminded to truly thank God for my celibacy. I saw that celibacy was not just about enduring a lack of sex but about being a sign of that heavenly future.

Yes, right now my surrendered same-sex desires were painful. But through that pain, God was revealing his glory. Without it,

I could never understand my deeper need for intimacy through friendships that pointed to Christ.

OVERCOMING FEAR AND REJECTION

The struggle in my heart over what had happened with Mark still raged. It was so far short of that vision of being a sign of heaven. One day, after reading in my quiet time about Jesus and the Beloved Disciple, I decided to go find Mark. I wanted to tell him about what I had been learning and to try to repair the unspoken breach in our friendship.

"David, sorry, but I'm in the middle of my evening," he said as he came out of his building and met me. "Is everything okay?" I could tell by his tone he was slightly annoyed.

My words came out in a rush. "Mark, I know we haven't been close since that day in the park. I've been thinking about it, and I think God has revealed something really important to me. I really think he's calling us into a beloved friendship. You know, like Jesus and John, or David and Jonathan. All this work at Oxford—everything we're learning about theology and ministry—all of it's worthless without these kinds of friendships."

He studied me. "What do you mean?"

I swallowed. "Well, I've been thinking about the relationship Jesus and John had, and I really want to know that kind of friendship with someone. I think that's what God has been inviting us into."

"David, let me cut this short. I don't really do that kind of intimacy with other men."

His words were like a bullet to my chest.

"Okay. I see. Well, I'd better leave you to your evening, then."

I turned and left in tears. All the old rejection flooded me, only worse because of the hope I had that maybe, *maybe,* there was real human acceptance for me.

That night, I tossed and turned, sleepless into the morning hours. As I listened to a nightingale sing outside my window, I wondered if Mark may have been afraid I was attracted to him and was trying to pass off a romantic attraction with a false request for friendship. If so, perhaps his fears as a straight male were more profound than his affections for me as a friend. For many weeks we didn't see each other, and it seemed our friendship was all but lost.

Months later I was surprised to discover I had developed feelings for Mark that were no longer platonic, even though I was not particularly attracted to him. Another battle in my war of loves was brewing. *What's going on?* I wondered. *Was this whole thing really all about lust all along?*

I look back now and wonder if I really know what was going on in my heart. But the more I consider the situation, the more deeply I feel that I was sincere—there was a call to deep friendship here, separate from any romantic involvement.

As I consider it now, I think I was trying to alleviate my sense of rejection by using sexual feelings. Lust was my attempt to define and control intimacy on my own terms and to put it back in familiar territory. It had very little to do with Mark himself.

Like so many in our day, I ran to the counterfeit god of sexuality for meaning, instead of seeking God for love, identity, intimacy, and satisfaction. As C. S. Lewis says, "It would seem that our Lord finds our desires not too strong, but too weak. . . . We are far too easily pleased." I had to learn to find acceptance in God.

Henri Nouwen observed something similar in his own life: "I kept running around it in large or small circles, always looking for someone or something able to convince me of my Belovedness. Self-rejection is the greatest enemy of the spiritual life because it contradicts the sacred voice that calls us the 'Beloved.' Being the Beloved expresses the core truth of our existence."[29]

I resonated with his words, because I too was repeating this cycle, and I longed to break free. But hope glimmered on the horizon. God was going to show me that I had been made for a higher love than physical intimacy, and that in order to try to experience it, I had to give up my control mechanism of selfish sexual desire.

One Sunday, the pastor at our church invited us to the trial run of a course on inner healing. He believed that false images of God were at the root of many of our emotional and psychological problems, and he had paired theology and psychology to address them. He explained to us how our perception of who God is needs to be corrected by Jesus, the image of the invisible God. Only then can we freely experience the Father's true love and intimacy through the Holy Spirit.

To my surprise, Mark was also taking the class. I knew I had to confess my attractions to him to recover our friendship. And yet I so wanted him to know that my original offer of covenant friendship never came from these attractions. Would he trust me?

As we took the seven-week course together, the pastor paired us up. Two broken men from very different backgrounds, one gay and one straight, were learning under Rabbi Jesus to really love each other by laying down their lives and identities for a friend. We both admitted our faults to each other. I told him about the reality of my attractions.

"David, I'm relieved you just owned up to your struggle," Mark told me earnestly. "I needed to hear that you were aware of how our friendship could have been compromised. I was worried you were either unaware of the possibility or trying to hide it. Now that I know what your real intentions are, I'm sorry I pushed you away."

After we shared, we each went off to a prayer counselor who had been assigned to us. In prayer, I felt God say to me, *David, I need you to be like a newborn child in my arms—no defenses and completely exposed before me. Let go of your control and let me* really *hold you.*

I became aware of another wall between myself and God that I had not known existed. Some deep part of me still believed I wasn't loved by God because of my struggle with sexuality. The orphan-hearted part of me both longed for and pulled away from the love of its Father.

Suddenly it felt like the Holy Spirit rushed over me. As Mark and I prayed with our separate prayer counselors at opposite corners of the room, I could feel the Spirit knocking on the door of my heart. *Let me in. Stop resisting.* Anger because of my perceived abandonment and rejection by God came pouring out of me. I realized that only the Father's adoptive love could free me from my sense of rejection.

There, in that eternal moment, I surrendered afresh, and God the Father held me like a baby in his arms. I realized again how tender and loving God the Father was! He was so different from the false perception I had once had of him as an angry old man. He was close. He was kind. He was good and tenderhearted.

My false image of God was broken, and with it went the false image of myself. I knew the Father's love in substance, not just theory. I was my Abba Father's, and he was mine.

Tears soaked my sweater and scarf. As we came out of prayer, I had a wad of used tissues in my hands. The man praying for me hadn't uttered a word but told me he heard the conversation I'd had with God. For a moment, he blinked in surprise; then we laughed together as joy from the deep healing I had just experienced hit me.

Later that night, walking in the low glow of Oxford's streetlamps, Mark and I made our way back to college knowing we had regained our friendship.

Weeks later at a conference in Oxford, I organized a prayer meeting. A professor who was a woman of prayer joined me, Mark, and many others as we interceded for one another. At the end of the meeting, she looked at Mark and said, "I have a word for you from the Lord. He is inviting you into a friendship with David that is like King David and Jonathan, and Jesus and John."

Both Mark and I were amazed that God spoke so directly through her, and I was relieved by his confirmation of what I had heard from him earlier. After this, in the security of God, Mark and I confidently committed to a covenant friendship that continues to bless us immensely today. At last, I was tasting something, in part, of what I had so long desired.

CHAPTER 23

LIVING OUT NOW

Carry each other's burdens, and in this way you will fulfill the law of Christ.

—*Galatians 6:2*

Living as a celibate gay/SSA Christian has been a huge challenge. I have experienced disgruntlement, prejudice, and social avoidance on both sides of our polarized culture and church. Many have accepted me, of course, but I always feel that, while I have never had a pink triangle pinned to my shirt like Brazda, the reality of my situation—choosing in obedience to Christ to be celibate—is something for which, for better or worse, I have often been judged in and outside the church.

It often seems, from my vantage point, that the gay rights movement isn't always interested in the rights of all gay people but rather is interested in the rights of the majority who believe in same-sex marriage. If there were real diversity and concern for everyone within the gay community, there would be acceptance of those like me and the churches that agree with my choice to embrace celibacy.

When celibate gay Christians choose to share publicly in the church, we are bombarded from all sides. We are asked to justify and explain ourselves. The constant questioning and pressure is exhausting.

Most progressives reject celibacy as a good or default choice for those who are gay or have same-sex desire. They do not see it as a necessary step in discipleship. To them, being gay requires sexual expression or romantic relationships, and our inner nature is a better guide to how we should live than the revelation of Christ in Scripture.

Some conservatives, or traditionalists, often refuse to love and move out toward the gay community, preaching that repentance means requiring gay people to erase their history and identity. Many on the conservative side of the church do not like that I appreciate much of the human rights work done by the gay rights movement. The reality is, I wouldn't have the freedom to write this book without the hard-fought progress achieved by that movement.

Another common criticism I've received is that I've made homosexuality my ultimate identity by calling myself a celibate gay (or SSA) Christian. This is deeply frustrating. It ignores the reality that I have died to my same-sex desires by submitting them to the lordship of Christ and choosing celibacy. My sexual orientation is a profound part of my story, and it is the very weakness that gives God unique glory because I live my life by faith in his Son. Many Christians don't understand that the terms same-sex attraction and homosexuality have questionable backgrounds for most gay people because they are linked to harmful therapies that attempted to cure homosexuals. There is no perfect term.

Both sides make our sexual lives the most important reality rather than focusing on eternal realities and how those impact our walk with Christ. But I cannot wait for progressive and conservative Christians to move on from this sinful divide. I have to live my life in Christ today, regardless of what the cultures around me choose or how we obsess about semantics.

Christians like me need to be held to the same standards as any other disciple and yet listened to and cared for in light of the particular challenges of being same-sex attracted. We need to die to ourselves just like everyone else and have our now-but-not-yet obedience affirmed by our church family. No Christian should carry a cross alone, and if someone is, the church is not fulfilling the law of Christ, as Paul talks about in Galatians 6:2.

Anglican theologian Sarah Coakley says that because the church is like a lightning rod for culture, the broader issues discussed in the culture concentrate in it.[30] The church in the West has been involved in a long and complex conversation about sexuality, which has not been very public, open, or positive for many.

This is nothing new. When the apostle Paul wrote to the various churches under his care, he saw how the Greek and Roman culture in their cities clashed with the culture of God's kingdom. The resulting issues distracted Christians from living under the lordship of Jesus. Paul struggled to establish a unified, Christ-centered, cross-based discipleship for those new Gentile followers.

Paul lovingly rebuked these communities and tried to integrate everything into Jesus Christ, his cross, and his resurrection. The Spirit inspired Paul's writings, and we still cherish them as our applicable, authoratitve guide. We see in these letters Paul's difficult wrestling with the various cultural challenges to the gospel. If it was hard for him, it is bound to be hard for us. Just like in Paul's time, the Christian challenge for us today is to renew our lives and experiences through Jesus Christ and his Word and the Spirit.

The Western church, however, has often failed to resist idolatry. In the last century, it has worshiped family above God and his kingdom, putting pressure especially on sexuality. In the postwar 1950s, the church made the nuclear family the idolatrous center of middle-class life. The 1960s reacted to this idolatry by throwing off the repression of desire and pursuing "free" sexuality. It brought its own set of idolatries.

In his book *The History of Sexuality,* French philosopher Michel Foucault attempted to uncover Western culture's trend of categorizing "deviant" forms of sexual desire, which were outside the societal normal of heterosexual marriage. Homosexuals were considered to be a separate class of person, akin to the "sodomite" in the medieval world. This reinvention of homosexual people as a perverse or deviant species meant that LGBTQI people lived in abject secrecy and fear for many years. In the 1950s and 1960s, medical speech described homosexuality as a dangerous perversity that threatened the utopic stability of the nuclear family.

Sadly, the church was influenced by these worldly ideas, which disciplined and punished those who reported no change in their sexual desires despite their efforts to eradicate them. The church and science colluded to try to cure gay people through all sorts of therapies (lobotomies and electroshock treatments are just a few). The terms same-sex attraction and homosexuality came out of this crucible.[31] This was not of the Holy Spirit and the kingdom of God but a tragic confusion and abuse of the reality of gay people.

We live in a time in the church when the facade has cracked, and we know these idolatrous ideas no longer work—indeed, never did. But my concern is that the church is capitulating to new pressures from today's culture. We are replacing old idolatries with new ones by developing prideful factions related to homosexuality, instead of repenting and seeking God in the unity of the Spirit and under the clear teaching of God's Word.

I pray each side will be willing to change or repent, to seek God's will alone, to preach the gospel to the world, and to make Jesus the center. Full stop.

SPEAKING OF SIDES

The "sides" terminology was developed by many in the LGBTQI Christian community and by the Gay Christian Network during the 2000s. Its purpose was to help people easily refer to their position on gay marriage and sexual expression. In the sides paradigm, there are four major camps among same-sex-attracted or LGBTQI Christians. (I have included these terms—I realize they are not perfect, but they can help us communicate differences quickly.)

- *Side A:* Disagrees with Christian tradition; affirms a gay identity and sees sexual expression in a gay marriage as faithful to a Christian ethic
- *Side B:* Affirms the Christian tradition that sees sexual expression in gay marriage as wrong, but incorporates gay identity under the lordship of Christ through celibacy and other forms of chastity
- *Side X:* Claims either to no longer experience same-sex attraction or to be ex-gay and to have been freed in the process of sanctification

- *Side Y:* Agrees with side B but does not identify with LGBTQI; prefers not to identify as gay but is more likely to use the term same-sex attracted or is reluctant to see sexual orientation as a category of identity or personhood

Side A groups affirm same-sex sexual expression in committed partnerships or marriages, while rejecting the sexually unrestrained tendencies of mainstream gay culture.

Those who identify as side B hold my perspective. Same-sex desire is seen as a complex entanglement of our very good humanity that is made for the intimate company of others and our fallen desires resulting from broken worship and the power of sin. These terms have real limitations, and for this reason I often use side B, same-sex attracted, *and* gay to talk about how I identify.

Side X refers to those who claim to no longer have same-sex attraction. Some claim this was through a form of ex-gay or reparative therapy, while others have arrived at this position through their own self-understanding and experience.

Side Y refers to those who repudiate any association with or identification as gay and describe themselves solely as same-sex attracted, distancing themselves from the LGBTQI movement.

Sadly, people from all of these sides most of the time do very little together. While we have important differences, we choose to fight each other instead of humbly hearing one another. It took me three years before I was willing to submit to God's clear teaching in Scripture. Instead, we have created our own churches and denominations, rejecting each other, our own lives, and our social media spheres. However, the biblical model when there is controversy or even disobedience to the gospel is to meet together, humbly removing both bitterness toward others and our idols, loving our enemies. In so doing, we are able to come to one mind, reaching a clear resolution through submitting to the authority of God's Word by the Holy Spirit. We see this in the Jerusalem Council in Acts 15, when the leaders of the church met to rule on God's adoption of the Gentiles and the place of the law in their newfound Christian identity. The real reformation cannot be a sidestepping of God's revealed word on sexuality but a gracious and passionate embrace of it above and beyond our identites, histories, or politics.

SIDE A AND PROGRESSIVE IDOLATRIES

From my perspective, the side A movement of LGBTQI Christians is founded on revisionist readings of the Bible that often are based on queer theology and queer theory. The starting point is human experience and a different place than the revelation of Jesus Christ and his God-breathed scriptures upon which Christian theology is based. They start from the experiences of LGBTQI people on the margins of theological or social scientific understanding and resist the ignorance that has oppressed them.

So what drives side A Christians? They often have a sincere and profound wish to reconcile God's call to chastity with the real experience of same-sex desire. To them, requiring all gay people to be celibate is absurd. (The difficulty here is that queer theology others gay or same-sex attracted celibacy by its own logic, since those who pursue celibacy are now the ones on the margins of the LGBTQI community!) Side A often (although not always) depicts Christians on the traditional side like me as being able to choose only "bad" celibacy or mixed-orientation marriages (a marriage between two people of the opposite sex, in which one or both spouses are otherwise attracted to the same sex).

According to the progressives, marriage must be extended to gay couples in the church so there can be social and theological affirmation of their partnerships and so they can experience God's sacramental blessing. I truly understand why, at all costs, progressive believers want their partnerships to be celebrated as marriages in the church. I say this because I was a side A Christian for three years, and I deeply empathize with their views.

As I've said already, side A worships the same idol of marriage that many on the traditional end do. They view sex and marriage as the place where true intimacy is found and see a lack of it as a deprivation of our humanity. That is something, they claim, Jesus would not ask of us.

The reality is, Jesus' call of discipleship is a claim on *all* of our lives. It is a lie that if gay people can't have marriage in the church, we will never be loved and accepted and affirmed as people but will be left as half-life humans, denied the chance to fully flourish that marital sexual expression ultimately provides.

SIDE B AND TRADITIONAL IDOLATRIES

Unfortunately, the side B world has its own (similar) idolatries. When people are wounded or even abusively treated by church leadership or the cultural war, we can be tempted to run to our own idolatries for comfort and identity. We often cling to our personal ideas instead of simply focusing on what it means to be a disciple of Christ.

The risk is that more progressive side B Christians judge

more traditional ones, and vice versa. Those in the side B world risk elevating their own individual theologies of sexuality, instead of valuing difference and fidelity to God.

The side B world can sometimes become so focused on its own predicaments that it forgets the wider kingdom mission of Jesus Christ. Chastity can become the point or goal of our lives, a constant gravitational obsession, instead of worshiping and enjoying Christ and living our lives of discipleship in deference to his lordship in the broader community of his church.

There is also a tendency sometimes, although it has been frequently disuaded, to elevate friendship and intimacy to an unhealthy level. While I absolutely affirm the church's vital need for non-nuclear, spiritual families and a strong culture of friendship, and while we are taught by Jesus Christ to have beloved friendship with others, no friendship can entirely provide for our needs. God provides primarily through his Spirit and only secondarily through others. As Augustine teaches, we are to enjoy God through all things and people.[32] That doesn't mean codependency; rather, it means dependency on God.

THE SOLUTION: IN CHRIST

When preaching at a large, multisite church in the United States, I met a young gentleman called David. He told me his story and about his parents, a loving and accepting evangelical couple whom he'd come out to at the age of fifteen.

After the service we sat and talked. He looked at me with a furrowed brow and said, "It's just not fair that as Christians, we have to give up any prospect of a romantic relationship with the person we're attracted to! Everyone else has the option of marriage. I don't. I want to have a family. I want a partner and children. Why can everyone else have that and I can't?"

I deeply identified with David's questions. In him, I saw reflections of my younger self. But I also saw that he, along with countless others in the church, had fallen prey to our culture's idolatry of romantic love. To him, the litmus test of human flourishing was sexual expression in marriage.

"I *completely* understand the cry of your heart, David," I told him. "I felt the same way for many years and wrestled through this with God."

I went on to explain that I am actually grateful for being gay or SSA, because it means I can no longer worship the gods of our culture. I am barred from their temples.

"I was told for so long that my sexual desires were what defined my humanity. But as a Christian, I learned that giving ourselves to God completely and trusting him with our same-sex desires is precious in his eyes. It helps us see that he is our greatest treasure and what we are really longing for. The goal of our lives isn't to fulfill our culture's expectations and worship our own desires but to follow Jesus and worship God. I have given up a portion of myself. But in return, I found my whole humanity."

"I'd never thought about it like that," David said slowly. "You're saying being same-sex attracted is sort of like an opportunity to really worship God?"

"Yes, that's right," I replied. "In reality, we have only fifty years or so to worship God this way. It's hard but so worth it. There's a reason Jesus said to Thomas, 'Blessed are those who believe and do not see.' But someday, in the new creation, we will see God in front of us. We won't have to trust him with desires like this, because all the effects of sin will have left us. We'll worship God with every fiber of our being because he'll fill every part of us."

The very legitimate fear of giving our everything to Christ is the greatest enemy to discipleship. We fail to recognize that every part of us, not just our sexuality, is baptized into the love of God. Incredibly, he then says, "Have yourself back again, in the way that will truly fulfill you."

Would you be willing to give up brother, mother, sister, or gay partner for the sake of God's kingdom? As Christians, we must be willing to give up anything to follow God. Jesus says to us, as he said to the church in Sardis, "So, because you are lukewarm—neither hot nor cold—I am about to spit you out of my mouth" (Rev. 3:16). Not one thing can be between us and him, or there will always be disunity. It follows, then, that in the church, unity cannot be achieved between those disciples who say, "Jesus, I submit my whole life to you" and those who don't. Ours is the common call, not some exotic one.

The reformation we all need is "in Christ," allowing every part of us—every desire, hope, and longing—to enter into his reality. This is an act of precious worship, like the sinful woman's act of pouring perfume on Christ's feet (Luke 7:36–50). I pray and hope all Christians, especially the "young Davids," would have this revealed to them.

PART 5

REFLECTIONS ON HOMOSEXUALITY AND CHRISTIAN FAITHFULNESS

CHAPTER 24

CELIBATE, GAY, CHRISTIAN: A THIRD WAY

> I have been crucified with Christ. It is no longer I who live, but Christ who lives in me. And the life I now live in the flesh I live by faith in the Son of God, who loved me and gave himself for me.
>
> —*Galatians 2:20 ESV*

The church needs a new apologetic, a way of thought and life that neither demonizes nor elevates the same-sex desires facing many faithful Christians. For this to happen, our minority living in the tension of grace and truth needs to speak up. Our experiences and stories are valuable and ought to be stewarded for our brothers and sisters to understand us.

This new apologetic must further permit us to form a deeper Christian response to homosexuality, one that honors both Scripture, the wisdom of tradition, *and* people's real experience. At the same time, such a response needs to recognize that we are waiting, that one day our final redemption will come and a great horizon of heavenly intimacy will be opened to us in Christ and his church, but that day has not yet fully dawned.

Let me sketch seven reasons why I hold to this position.

The first is *scriptural authority*. While Scripture is clear that homosexual acts are sinful, it also maintains that Christians live in tension between the fallen nature, or "flesh," that is at war with God, and the new self, which desires to love and obey God. When we become born again, our old nature is crucified with Christ, but it is also still present, as we feel painfully in moments of temptation or testing. Presently, our victories in Christ are manifested in weakness, not in the strength of resurrected bodies.

The apostle John holds these two realities in tension. "If we claim to be without sin, we deceive ourselves and the truth is not in us," he says (1 John 1:8). Later he speaks of God's sanctifying power: "No one born of God makes a practice of sinning, for God's seed abides in him; and he cannot keep on sinning, because he has been born of God" (1 John 3:9 ESV).

Commenting on 1 Corinthians 6:9–11, J. I. Packer writes with remarkable clarity about Paul's gospel: "With some of the Corinthian Christians, Paul was celebrating the moral empowering of the Holy Spirit in heterosexual terms; with others of the Corinthians, today's homosexuals are called to prove, live out, and celebrate the moral empowering of the Holy Spirit in homosexual terms."[33]

The Holy Spirit's moral empowerment in the midst of our present struggles with sin is what leads many of us to call ourselves celibate gay Christians. To say, "I've been healed from all temptations of the flesh" is to make the same error the Corinthians did when they thought they were already without a fallen nature, and yet behind closed doors were still indulging in sinful behaviors.

The scholar Anthony Thiselton coins it "over-realized eschatology,"[34] meaning an expectation of heavenly perfection while still in this world. Sorry. It's still hard.

On the flip side, to deny that God will not presently give us victory over sinful desires is to commit the error of "under-realized eschatology," which causes us to live in slavery to sin without hope of any real freedom from it in this life.

But here's the truth: Christians, *all* Christians, are being made holy. We aren't yet perfect. We still experience the attractions of our old self. Yet because of Christ, we can live in victory. God does not wave a magic wand to remove our desires—at least, that is not the normative experience. It is equally wrong to endorse or to deny the presence of fallen desires, and that is why I call myself a gay or same-sex-attracted *celibate* Christian.

My second reason is *theological accuracy*. For the gay or same-sex-attracted person, a biblical understanding of what it means to be redeemed is complex. To be attracted to the same sex is not a voluntary behavior, as many have incorrectly argued. Instead it is a result of the creation-wide effects of sin. Wesley Hill, a New Testament professor and celibate gay Christian, states, "Many suggest that a parallel case would be if someone were to label himself an 'adulterous Christian' or a 'stealing Christian.' Those terms are self-evidently problematic in that they make sinful behaviors part of an identity description for believers, and therefore gay Christians should find their chosen label equally problematic. My response to this is that those are not, in fact, parallel cases."[35]

The word gay does not necessarily refer to sexual behavior; it can just as easily refer to one's sexual preference or orientation and say nothing, one way or the other, about how one is choosing to *express* that orientation. So, whereas "stealing Christian" describes a believer who actively steals as an acted behavior, "gay Christian" may simply refer to one's orientation and nothing more.

This is why I rarely, if ever, use the phrase gay Christian without adding the adjective celibate, meaning committed to a life of chasteness in Christ. To call myself a celibate gay Christian specifies both my sexual orientation *and* the way I'm choosing to live it out.

We have all been impacted by the fall. The particular challenge for the majority of gay or same-sex-attracted Christians is untangling the sinful aspect of same-sex attraction from their God-given desire for intimacy. Some find that this need for human intimacy is met in celibate friendships; a smaller group report a special God-given attraction to a particular opposite-sex partner in a mixed-orientation marriage. But most side B Christians choose celibacy.

Very few same-sex-attracted or gay people report that when they become Christians, their desires simply disappear. Rather, as in my story, many find that God gives them a special empowering grace to be celibate. That is our experience.

Many of those pressured by Christian culture to say they have been healed live with secret sexual sin and shame as a result of their desires actually not going away, or even intensifying by being locked away out of sight. We must break the culture of silence in many churches and instead encourage a culture of repentant honesty before God and with each other. Anything else will allow spiritual darkness to deepen, grieving the Spirit of truth.

My third reason is to be *prophetic*. Those of us who are orthodox or traditional Christians and who are gay or SSA need to reclaim our space in the conversation over sexuality back from the secular culture. While we have shared experience of same-sex desires with those who are gay and seek to be in gay marriages, including dealing with them in a fallen world that is prejudiced and unloving, we are different, and this needs to be reflected in how we understand what it means to be gay or SSA in broader society. Also, people like me have benefited from the gay rights movement in many ways and would not be able to live the open life we do without many of these wins for human dignity, but we don't want that movement to spell the deprivation of our rights to live in churches that support our choices and obedience to Christ. We can identify with many of its wins for the human dignity of LGBTQI/SSA people, including employment rights, protections from hate crimes, and antidiscrimination laws, even if we may disagree on sexual ethics. We have the unique opportunity to break a culture of victimhood toward traditional Christians, as well as gay/SSA people.

The opposite of homosexuality is not heterosexuality. It is *holiness*. We need to stand for a different way to live in the gay community, and welcome others from that community into the church to receive Jesus' love, without denying so many of the goods won through the gay rights movement.

The fourth reason is related to *identity*. When Christians receive Christ, we repent of what is sinful. But we don't renounce our individual humanity, which is shaped both by God and by our experience in this fallen world and this fallen body. As a gay celibate Christian, I recognize that Christ is my ultimate identity; gay and celibate come second. My identity is first and foremost in Christ, but those other two descriptors tell the redemptive story of God's grace in my life.

When I chose to be celibate, I placed the word gay under the lordship of Christ; it is no longer a competitive identity to "in Christ" but a beautiful reminder of my submission to his lordship over my whole life, including my sexuality.

My fifth reason is *reconciliatory*. Like God, who became human in Christ and reached out across our human experience, we must learn to love others, made in the image of God, by identifying and entering into their experience. Part of that involves learning their language and regarding it with sacred importance so we can love our neighbors and our enemies.

Christians have built a prejudiced stereotype and generalization of the gay community. Promiscuity and sexual orientation must be separated in our thinking. I came to know Jesus when I was heavily involved in the gay rights movement, and I know firsthand that not everything in the gay community is licentious or wrong.

There is a distinction between the gay scene, which can often be commercialized and sexually libertine, and the gay community, which is composed of all people who experience same-sex desires. Christians need a more nuanced and sensitive understanding when they use the word gay.

The gay community is made up of people who are loved by God and need to be told about the love of Christ and the gospel. Are Christians willing to reach out to and enter our world to share and connect? This will always be a two-way discovery. Will Christians be like Jesus, who put the taboo of his day to one side and loved the Samaritan woman, arguably one of the most morally questionable people in his context and time?

Some of us have sinfully failed to reach out to, value, and love the gay community but are very happy to moralize and judge. This is far removed from the radical holiness and truth, on one side, and compassion and mercy, on the other, that Jesus showed to "outsiders." His example leads the way for us.

My sixth reason is *reformative*. Paul was a Jew. That identity he was born with was an integral part of his life and his relationship with Messiah Jesus. However, his view of Judaism and how he related to it changed. It was always part of his identity but was no longer his primary identity. He was now in Jesus, and that changed how he related to Judaism. (Still, his Jewish identity and history gave him the ability to speak about Christ to Jews scattered throughout the Roman world!)

My seventh and final reason is *invitational*. Mainstream secular culture feels alienated by terms like same-sex attracted and gay lifestyle. There is no monolithic gay lifestyle. The term same-sex attracted sounds medical, like a diagnosis—reminiscent of when same-sex desire was seen as a disease. Such terms can place hindrances in the way of those who need to hear the gospel message. When I entered the church and heard these terms, they kept me from feeling included and understood.

On the other hand, the term gay is positive and welcoming for those who are gay or SSA. Christians would do well to focus on removing boundaries—existential, intellectual, and spiritual—in order to know the good news for our own sexual brokenness, and then, further, to share the good news humbly from this place with others.

Identifying with others in the LGBTQI world can open doors to engage people who need to hear about Christ. It can also give us the chance to speak honestly against the horrible ways Christians have often treated the gay community. I pray this third-way apologetic will carry us out of the harmful culture war and into the new frontiers of reaching people for Christ.

CHAPTER 25

SPEAKING TRUTH IN LOVE

> Any theory divorced from living examples . . . is like an unbreathing statue.
>
> —*Gregory of Nyssa*

> Speaking the truth in love, we will grow to become in every respect the mature body of him who is the head, that is, Christ.
>
> —*Ephesians 4:15*

> "For this reason a man will leave his father and mother and be united to his wife, and the two will become one flesh." This is a profound mystery—but I am talking about Christ and the church.
>
> —*Ephesians 5:31–32*

I was coming to the end of my first year of studies at Oxford. Over the last weeks of my ethics classes, I had been asking deeper questions about why God originally created sexual differences, and how sin and death had affected those differences.

I befriended many people at Oxford who were transgender,

and one person who was intersex, and was deeply saddened by their stories of being treated horribly by Christians. They didn't fit into the gender-binary view held by most people, including those in the church. Rather than seeing these people and their broken bodies and desires through the lens of Jesus Christ, Christians tended to view them through broken understandings of sexuality and gender.

I had so many questions raised by these relationships. Was a broken heterosexual marriage not centered on Christ superior to a transgender couple seeking Christ for their new lives? Was a Christian view of masculinity that excluded people who didn't fit the stereotype really any better than a view that exalted gay sexual identity above Jesus' call to discipleship?

I did not know all the answers. I still don't. These are hard questions. But I knew that all of us in the church need a deeper desire to know God and hear from him on these issues. Our present realities of gender and fallen sexual desire need to be interpreted through humanity's future redemption in Jesus Christ.

Without knowing Jesus and dying to our old selves, we cannot experience being a new creation. We are slaves, stuck between unrestrained sexual expression and restrictive repression of our desires. Christians also still experience the effects of sin and the fall. But when we become new creations in Christ, God renews our desires and minds through Jesus' resurrection power. This new creation will be completed only when we are raised bodily from the dead. That means our current bodies, which are groaning for renewal, are not our ultimate reality! Our resurrection bodies will far surpass this fallen creation, and their desiring will be righteous.

I had always wavered on my theology of marriage, even as I came to my own personal conclusions. Was what I was personally called to normative? At Oxford, I had paced the stacks of those "beautiful old libraries" Leon had seen, searching for answers.

I pored over Scripture and the writings of Augustine, Karl Barth, Dietrich Bonhoeffer, Sarah Coakley, and many of the church Fathers. I came to understand the profound theological meaning of marriage in the church, and God's revealed purposes for human sexuality became clearer. While I still respected the right of all people to have their monogamous relationship protected by the state, I could no longer support same-sex unions in the church. Appeals to our human experience were not enough to convince me. God's vision for marriage was profound and beautiful. I could not dismiss it.

I knew God was calling me to lovingly *accept* but not *affirm* all relationships. My goal was to point toward a fundamental reality: the marriage of Christ and his bride, the church. My doctrine needed to be informed by Jesus' love for his bride, reflected in God's creation of us as male and female.

Some will say marriage is a mere metaphor. It is a metaphor, surely, but it's more than that too. It is, as Paul says, a profound mystery, something we will not understand fully until it is fulfilled in God's kingdom. But one day, it is promised, we will understand it perfectly. We will receive the reality it points us to.

As part of my training at Oxford, I was required to take part in missions at universities around the United Kingdom. When I arrived at one university to support a mission with the Christian Union, I saw posters for an interfaith discussion about gay marriage. Many of my Christian friends there strongly discouraged me from attending, but I decided to go and bring with me a bisexual friend who was also dedicated to giving her desires to Christ.

When we arrived, my heart was pounding. This was the first time in years I had engaged directly with gay activists, but I was excited to share with others my view of marriage. We entered the small brick building and sat in a circle with twenty-five people of different faiths and backgrounds.

A blond man, who described himself as a gay activist, opened the meeting. He reminded me so much of myself from several years before. "We have purposefully held this conversation to hear all of your perspectives on gay marriage, especially as it relates to your faith," he said, smiling. "This is a safe space to share."

Despite his warm welcome, the room was tense. It seemed many in the group were nervous. But as we went around the room, there were no dissenting viewpoints. Every person, whether they were from a Sikh, Muslim, Jewish, or some other background, said they had no problem with gay sexual expression and supported gay marriage.

The time came for me to speak. My heart was still pounding, but an inner peace was there too. I knew I had to be honest about my views, or this dialogue would have lacked the wider perspectives it was supposed to cultivate. It was a safe space, right? And I genuinely loved these people.

"Well, this may not be popular in this room," I said, "but as a gay/same-sex-attracted celibate Christian, I do not believe gay sexual expression is right for me."

The room went silent. Several people recoiled from my words, then looked at me as if I were an alien.

I proceeded to briefly tell my story, then grinned at them. "I even have a personal hashtag. It's #fabulousmadeglorious!"

Everyone in the room laughed. Their posture changed from defensive to open.

"I believe God made our bodies. They matter—matter so much that God became human in Jesus. The fact that God created human beings with two sexes reveals he values both the diversity and unity of human persons, not because he wants to condemn LGBTQI people!" I paused and looked around the circle. "For Christians, marriage between the male and female sexes takes on a deeper meaning only when we understand the relationship of Jesus, who's the Bridegroom, and the church, who's his bride.

"God has called me to trust that he knows best and he knows the eternal story he's writing. In the meantime, he's shown me I can give my same-sex desires to him and find a deeper satisfaction and love in knowing and worshiping him than I ever could through pursuing my desires."

As I said this, people seemed to understand what I was trying to communicate. The gay activist who opened the meeting broke the silence after I shared. "Well, I suppose sex does get a bit old after a while!"

"But worship doesn't!" I replied.

"I suppose not," he said, and the whole room laughed again.

I was grateful to this young activist for respecting my journey. I knew he understood the struggle I had been through. Even if he did not agree with my conclusions, he didn't dismiss me as not truly gay or not part of the community but respected that I wanted to live differently in Christ. His friendly words were one of the greatest kindnesses I had received from the LGBTQI community since my choice to surrender my same-sex desires to Jesus.

Before we finished, I felt compelled to share something more. "If I could leave everyone in this room with one message, it's that human marriage between one man and one woman is just a reflection of a more fundamental marriage. That's the one between Jesus and his church. There is no sexual or gender minority group, no religious group, that's not invited to his wedding."

God worked through it. When I finished, several people were crying. While most of the LGBTQI people there disagreed with my conclusion, they thanked me for sharing so honestly. Some people from other faiths admitted to me that they did not have the courage to share their deeper views, because they didn't want to be perceived as homophobic and unloving. I had managed to be honest without being judgmental. Little did they know the years of work and tears it had taken to get to that place in my own heart. I left that meeting eager for more. I had a real hope now that peaceful, honest exchanges could be possible. Several people who were at this meeting attended our Christian Union events days afterward. Eventually some even came to know Jesus Christ for themselves, each with a remarkable, beautiful story of their journey to faith.

Unless we learn how to accept others without affirming everything, we have lost the art of conversation, because we're suppressing our honest opinions. We can accept and affirm people without agreeing with and affirming *all* of their desires or beliefs or accepting their actions.

Jesus was teaching me that I could offer both love and truth as I shared my story.

You see, love without truth is not love at all.

And truth without love?

Well, it's not truth.

CHAPTER 26

SACRIFICE REGAINED: SALVATION AND HOLINESS

Because your love is better than life, my lips will glorify you.

—Psalm 63:3

You are what you worship. And you worship what you love.

—James K. A. Smith

The Sunday afternoon rain ran down the windowpane to the sill. My phone vibrated.

A text—from a French number.

Hey, David, it's Jerome!
Long time no see! I'm in Oxford.
Can I see you?

My heart skipped a beat. I wondered whether it was wise to text back. The last time I'd seen Jerome was two years ago when I'd broken things off in Strasbourg.

I set out for my friend's room down the hallway and asked her what she thought. I found her sketching a new painting. "Yeah—probably not wise," she said, after I filled her in on the situation.

I left my friend to her art and went back to my room to pray. Strangely, I felt that I should respond, even though I was nervous about what it would bring up in me. *Go, David. You're ready for this,* I felt God whisper to me. *I will be with you.*

Much had changed in two years. I loved my life, this new way of living in Jesus Christ. My existence was far richer than I'd expected. I decided I could meet Jerome without compromising my faith. I just needed to be careful. I remembered those eyes. *Really careful.* I texted him back, friendly but very careful to avoid any hint of flirtation (harder than it sounds when composing a text message). We picked a nearby café to meet.

When the time approached, I pushed open my building's heavy oak door and said a short prayer. "Thank you, Lord. Help me show Jerome who you are."

A spring storm had just passed. The fresh air whirled around me as I walked the streets. I was nervous but excited. I still had profound affections for Jerome and was struggling to push those aside. More than anything, I wanted this man to know Jesus Christ.

When I entered the coffee shop, the French band Air was playing over the speakers. Nostalgia hit me like the smell of a Strasbourg bakery. Jerome was in the corner. His face, with its wide cheekbones, dark ruddy stubble, and wide-framed glasses, hadn't changed a bit. We sat over hot drinks.

Time flew by. There was a lot to catch up on. As we chatted in French, he told me about his time studying political science in Canada. I asked if I could show him around Oxford, and he readily agreed. We walked out into the lovely afternoon.

As we passed the blooming flowers of the university parks, I decided to take him to one of my new favorite spots, Keble College Chapel. We entered the brick building and paused by William Holman Hunt's famous painting *The Light of the World,* which hangs in a side crypt of the old chapel. The painting is an image of Jesus—his eyes enigmatic, distant almost—holding a lantern in a twilight garden, standing by a door with no handle. It is lush, cryptic, beautiful.

"The door has no handle because Hunt was making a point about how we need to make a decision about who Jesus is," I told Jerome. "He's always waiting on the other side of the door to welcome us into the new creation he started through the cross and in his resurrection. We all have the choice of whether we'll let Jesus come in and eat with us or not. Jesus never forces us to open our hearts. We have to let him in."

He nodded silently and looked around in awe. "I didn't know faith like this existed," he said.

As we wound our way back through the center of Oxford, I had one last stop in mind—Christ Church. I flashed my student card to see if the librarian would also allow us into the college's library. Usually only members of the college were permitted inside, but it was one of my absolute favorite libraries in Oxford. The exterior was bordered with thick Roman columns. The inside was white, with quintessentially Georgian features. Spiral staircases wound up to neat collections of books, split into sections. I took Jerome up one of the staircases to a ledge by the philosophy and theology collection. It was out of view, a place I often frequented.

Jerome looked up at the ceilings and open windows and took in the golden letters of the dusty book titles. "This is beautiful."

Then my heart quickened, feeling that familiar energy of mutual attraction. Jerome leaned in slowly for a kiss.

I pulled back, though everything in me screamed not to. "David, are you sure you don't want this?" he said, taking my hand.

The thought of a life together passed through my mind, and my affections were stirred. I shook my head and gently let go of his hand. "No. I'm sure. I'm in love with Jesus Christ. My life is his and not my own," I said quietly.

He didn't try to argue but seemed resigned. "David, ever since I met you, you were different," he whispered in French. "I can't explain what it is about you. You're unique. You're not like the other guys I've met. But I don't understand why you keep denying yourself a relationship."

I shook my head again. "I feel deeply for you, Jerome. But I have to choose Jesus." I smiled at him. "I've given myself to God. *All* of me. Jesus has made a whole new world, and I'm beginning to be part of it. He's going to recreate everything, our bodies included. All of this"—I paused to look around me—"will be transformed. I want you to be part of *that* world, so we can enjoy God and each other forever. So no, I'm really not interested. But . . ." I smiled wryly. "I *did* want to ask you if you'd like to attend church with me tonight."

Jerome nodded. "I know there's something real behind your choice," he said. There was both disappointment and respect in his voice. "Of anyone I've met, you stand out. Your life says that Jesus is real and that he has a love that's—how do I say it—higher. So yes. I will come."

As we walked into my church, Jerome stopped and stared. The whole room reverberated with the sound of diverse Oxford City people singing praise to God at the top of their voices.

The sound poured out into the streets. Hundreds of students packed the seats. "If church was like this in France, I'd be there every Sunday!" Jerome whispered to me.

All my friends welcomed Jerome. A few people were perhaps wondering what I was doing with an attractive Frenchman, but I knew God was behind this meeting.

As we made our way to the bus stop to say goodbye, I could see that Jerome was visibly moved. "David, you're set apart *[consacré]* for God, aren't you?" he said in French. Consecrated! That was it. Exactly.

I was in awe that God was giving me this opportunity to share with Jerome. "Yes, that's right! Every Christian is supposed to be set apart for God. We're called to a higher love. The Bible calls it our first love. I've experienced that love from Jesus, and it's turned my life upside down."

His face lit up with both wonder and bewilderment. "You mean, you're never going to have a gay partner or sex? You'd give that up for God?"

I nodded. "Yes. God's worth that sacrifice any day."

I paused and looked intently at Jerome. "Would you think about following Jesus too? I would give anything to have you in eternity with me! We can share the love of Jesus now and for eternity. I love who you are as a person, Jerome. I wouldn't want a tiny lifetime of sexuality to get in the way of an eternity of friendship."

Jerome's bus pulled up. Our time was coming to a close. He hugged me. We both had tears in our eyes.

"David, if there's anyone I've ever met in my life who has made me seriously think about Christianity, it's you. When we were together in Strasbourg—that time in bed when you were touched by God—I've never been able to shake it. The love of God you have is special. It's worth protecting. I respect you for that. I want you to know that I don't see you as some repressed or self-hating celibate, like some people might say."

"Thank you, Jerome," I told him. "You can have the same love. Open up and you'll find Jesus there. He's knocking! Please don't worry about the sexuality thing. That will work itself out. Just let him in."

We hugged one last time. His face was full of joy as he gave me two final *bisous* on the cheek. Turning to climb the bus stairs, he said, "Thank you, David."

As the bus pulled away, I realized that Jerome had seen Jesus in me. I did not need to hide myself away from the world or complex situations. Rather I could face them with the help and power of Christ.

I believe that God graciously used holiness as the window through which Jerome could see the reality of a greater intimacy. Without holiness, none of us can see God or his love. There is a horizon so much wider than most of us have ever dreamed. Perhaps only a glimpse of that horizon can help people like Jerome understand that in their search for intimacy, what they really have been looking for is *Jesus*.

They have been knocking on the other side of the door depicted in William Holman Hunt's painting. At the same time, they have been unwilling to open it to Jesus. And the handle is on their side. He will not force himself on anyone.

When we come to Christ, the crucial question is what to do with our identity. The things that make up our identity are fundamental to our nature. They are what we're known for and validated for.

Atheist David Foster Wallace once said, "In the day-to-day trenches of adult life, there is actually no such thing as atheism. There is no such thing as not worshiping. Everybody worships."[36]

Whatever we worship shapes our identity. It could be sexuality, vocation, family, or gender. Whatever it might be, we were made to cleave to God for identity and meaning.

Oliver O'Donovan, former Regius Professor of Moral and Pastoral Theology at Oxford University, states, "If Christianity has a saving message to speak to human beings, it must surely be, 'You may be free from the constraints of your identities.'"[37]

When Jesus Christ is relegated to a hobby for middle-class families and not allowed to be the Lord of our entire lives, we are bound to destroy the witness of his gospel. What the Western church needs is a new identity that recognizes that Jesus isn't just a peripheral interest. He's the center of everything.

It should come as a great relief that we no longer have to be our own gods or be slaves to our old identities, including homosexuality. Compared with eternity, homosexuality is a momentary desire. It will soon pass away with God's new creation in Jesus Christ. The same goes with all other broken desires. The overriding reality is God's kingdom and our new identity in him.

The biblical story of Ruth, more than anything, has taught me this truth. Ruth was a Moabite woman, excluded from the covenant promises of Israel, but incredibly, she became part of the genealogy of Jesus Christ.

After the death of her husband, Ruth chose to remain faithful to her Israelite mother-in-law, Naomi, who was grieving the death of her husband and her sons. Together they journeyed back to Israel, where Ruth threw herself on the faithfulness of God and made him the center of her life. Then Boaz, a kinsmen-redeemer from Naomi's extended family, rescued Ruth from the poverty of being a widow, and Naomi from her childlessness. He covered Ruth with the hem of his garment, as a sign of betrothal.

Boaz is an image of Jesus, who redeems us from our old identities with his covenant love. On the cross, he covered us with the hem of his garment. This beautiful truth is reiterated in Ezekiel 16:8, which uses the same phrase from the book of Ruth: "I spread the corner of my garment over you and covered your naked body. I gave you my solemn oath and entered into a covenant with you, declares the Sovereign Lord, and you became mine."

This covering, or overshadowing, is a theme seen throughout Scripture. When Mary is told she will conceive a child, she is overshadowed by the Holy Spirit. On the Mount of Transfiguration, the Holy Spirit overshadows Jesus like a cloud, and God declares that Jesus is his beloved Son. At Pentecost, the church was born, empowered, and baptized with the Spirit. God poured out his covenant love on a great diversity of his children. From this point until today, those outside of Israel are being adopted into the family of God.

I came to see that God had covered me with the hem of his garment and pledged his covenant love to me as part of his bride, the church. He said to me, *David, you are not ultimately celibate, gay, or any of these titles or labels. While they are part of your reality now, the ultimate reality is that you are betrothed to me. My love is your true identity.*

While I still use the words gay and celibate to describe myself, what ultimately defines me is God's overshadowing covenant love. And he invites *all* people, including those like me, into this same holy, covering relationship.

LUKEWARM CHRISTIANS AND ANGRY ACTIVISTS

I am often asked by Christians, "What can we do to better love our LGBTQI neighbors?" While there are many issues that need serious attention, most of them stem from a Christian failure to really listen and love. Instead of creating a safe place for people like LGBTQI Christians to share, we tend to react from fear, not from the security of the gospel.

God wants *all* people everywhere to turn from their ways in order to know him. He wants us all to adopt an entirely different view of meaning, transcendence, and worship. Can you imagine how healing it would be for the church to acknowledge that it is just as broken and sinful as the gay community? Can you imagine the power in store if Christians were to humbly repent of hypocrisy before expecting others to repent?

When the church does not demonstrate radical discipleship that is willing and able to meet people where they are, it holds us all back. We become afraid to face head-on the questions that need to be answered if the church is to flourish and mature. Capitulating to secular culture's view of sexuality makes it hard for people like me to accept Jesus' claim on our lives.

A weak culture of friendship and fellowship excludes LGBTQI people and forces them to look for intimacy in the wrong places. We need a community life like the one modeled in Acts, in which believers lived as a new family in the light of Jesus' life and mission to the nations.

We must all humbly name that kind of life as what we want and be willing to pay the price for it to be a reality. We must all call for deeper restoration and renewal of the church. The question of sexuality must always be related to *actual people,* people who matter to the heart of Christ and the kingdom of God. When we can move beyond seeing homosexuality and same-sex desire as part of a culture war we must (or can) win, we may finally see the people behind the smokescreen of identity politics, truly loving them with the kind of love God has shown us.

What will this look like in action? It means we Christians must open up our private family lives and welcome others into the kind of spiritual families and intimate communities we see demonstrated in the book of Acts and the early church. It means that we must act like what we say we are: a new humanity in Jesus.

There are no easy solutions for LGBTQI people, and instead of acting like there are, we must help them carry their burdens, just as we would embrace or help any brother or sister. The church must be able to admit its weaknesses and moral failures, or else those who are gay, are celibate, have gender dysphoria, or identify as trans will simply not be able to belong. Any pride that shelters homophobia or infers heterosexual superiority is a sinful deterrent to LGBTQI people and has hindered the witness of the church. We need honesty, bravery, and openness to find the way of Jesus through this.

I often hear gay or progressive activists say that celibate gay Christians are the new ex-gay, referring to the harrowing history of conversion therapy. Or these activists call those who support us repressive. I need to name that for what it is: discrimination, and it is as deeply hurtful as any homophobia I experienced as a sexually active gay man.

Being gay is not about having gay sex. That is a moral choice separate from gay identity. Of all communities in the world, gay communities are well poised to accept and understand that distinction. I pray that they will.

TO BE AN ABRAHAM

In saving us, God does not erase us or our history. Rather, as our identities are brought under Christ's lordship, he makes us into who we were meant to be. When we cling to fallen desires more than to God, we miss out on the greater identity God has for us as his children. God's first commandment is to have no other gods before him, and this includes the false worship of our identities. If our love for God is real, every one of us must be willing to give up *anything* in response to his love so it can be transformed, including our sexuality. Without knowing the love of God, none of us can free ourselves from the identities that cruelly deprive us of true freedom.

In Genesis, we read the story of Abraham and Lot, two men to whom God revealed himself. The Scriptures declare that they were both righteous in God's sight. However, Abraham feared and obeyed God; Lot did not. These two men's lives were marked by different decisions in response to God's grace, love, and faithfulness.

When God called Abraham to leave a secure metropolis for a herding life in the wilderness, I am sure God's command seemed unwise and nonsensical. Likewise, to many, my choice to be celibate as a gay man looks strange and even offensive, as it would have looked to me before I met Christ. Others see it as a harmful form of self-denial.

To our natural minds, God's calling to obedience and holiness often appears foolish. Paul writes in 1 Corinthians that "the foolishness of God is wiser than human wisdom" (1:25) and that "God chose the foolish things of the world to shame the wise; God chose the weak things of the world to shame the strong"

(v. 27). The very cross of Jesus, as Paul states, is foolishness to the wise. We who carry it will be seen as foolish, but we have found the wisdom of true worship. We have found the way of God's love.

Like Lot, who chose to dwell in a pagan place at great cost, some trust the voice of today's human wisdom. "Sex is intimacy," that voice says. "You can't live without it. Live out your sexual desires the way you like. This is how God made you, and it's who you are!"

However, like Abraham, a small and brave group of people choose to listen to God's voice and follow it where it takes them. God freely offers the gift of salvation, but it's our choice whether to lay down our sexuality or any other hindrance, pick up our cross, and follow Jesus Christ. True faith is revealed in obedience and good works. We turn from sinfully worshiping our own attempts at working things out instead of loving God.

The question of whether a gay or same-sex-attracted person can be saved reflects a complete misunderstanding of the gospel of Jesus Christ. Of *course* they can be saved! The real question is, will gay or same-sex-attracted believers live the way the world encourages them to? Or will they give up their plans and desires to follow Jesus in celibacy or another arrangement he provides, even under the ridicule of friends, family, or some members of the church?

Those who choose Abraham's path of faith will be called great in the kingdom of heaven and inherit God's promises, but right now they tread a path of cultural, sexual, and social poverty. Knowing God in Jesus Christ and following him will cost us everything. Yet it is Jesus who leads us, and he promises us relational riches in the kingdom of heaven, both now and in the future. He will give us back infinitely more, today and in the age to come. I have found this to be true. The joy I have now far exceeds anything I knew in my past life.

Those who, like Lot, choose to live their own way face both an uncertain fate and dangerous consequences. The choice is ours. Will we receive this free gift of salvation but insist on controlling our own lives? Or will we follow Jesus wherever he takes us and allow him to define our choices? This is the ultimate war of loves. It is a war for our trust and for our worship.

Our entry into the kingdom of heaven is through faith. But faith without works is dead. One day, God's judgment of each of us will reveal whether our faith was genuine. God calls us to demonstrate our faith now, through his enabling power, by changing our minds, turning from our own way, and giving up everything to follow him.

God promises those who become sexually poor for the sake of his kingdom that, like the eunuchs in Isaiah 56, their name will be an eternal one, which is even better than having sons and daughters. This promise is especially precious for LGBTQI people. Our descendants will be as many as the stars. We will not be a dried-up old tree. We can be like the Ethiopian eunuch in Acts 8, who, according to church tradition, became the spiritual father of the whole continent of Africa. God promises the same glorious progeny in our obedience and in our trust in him. As Christ says in Matthew 6:33, "Seek first his kingdom and his righteousness, and all these things will be given to you as well." Whatever we give up we receive back in a far greater form.

By faith, Abraham trusted that God's reward was more vast than the star-filled sky above him. Abraham was even willing to offer up the future represented by his promised only son, when God told him to take Isaac up to Mount Moriah and sacrifice him, to test that he did not wrongly worship the gift above the giver. But instead, God the Father really did give up his Son for us! We are called, in response, to give up those things most precious to us, including our romantic lives and sexuality.

The love of God is fierce and says, "I will not leave you as orphans" (John 14:18). But it also says, "Pick up your cross and follow me!" (see Matt. 16:24). It's not a cheap love; it is a holy love that changes lives. As Dietrich Bonhoeffer said, "Cheap grace is the preaching of forgiveness without requiring repentance, baptism without church discipline, communion without confession. Cheap grace is grace without discipleship, grace without the cross, grace without Jesus Christ, living and incarnate."[38]

If our lives are not shaped by true grace, we will end up like Lot—broken, shamed, wasted. Every work done or choice made not in faith will be burnt up in God's purifying judgment and cannot be taken with us into eternal life. For the true follower of Jesus, it's never an option to live like Lot. The person transformed by God's grace *wants* to be and is an Abraham.

God's love, demonstrated on the cross two millennia ago, is not a license to live our own way. Jesus Christ bids us come and die and be resurrected. Whatever our sexual orientation, we all must die to our desires so we may be brought into the new life of God's kingdom. But we cannot do this until we know God's love. As in a human relationship of fidelity and faithfulness, we must lay down anything that gets in the way of our relationship with God. If we turn to him, he promises to make something beautiful from our brokenness.

Jesus said, "Whoever lives by believing in me will never die" (John 11:26). He offers this gift of eternal life to every person, even to an atheistic young activist in a pub in the gay quarter of Sydney. That is my story. I could die to my identity and my desires only when I knew God had given everything for me to know him.

Each of us is given a choice: will we escape our self-imposed death sentence by repenting and believing the incredibly good news that God loves us? Jesus Christ put an end to this war of loves between our idols and the true and living God. He stands ready to welcome us into his embrace, if we are willing to lay down our right to define ourselves.

The love of God is where each of us can find freedom from the prison of our own identity. This is what I have experienced. If my story has any message, it is that the love of God can reach any of us, wherever we are. That includes you. The question I was asked on the night I discovered Jesus is the same one I now pose to you: have you experienced the love of God?

The angry activist that I was, with my bitterness, desire for vengeance, and attempt to force the church to adopt my self-made ethic, was really trying to assert myself as lord over the church. In the same way, the real issue at the heart of our culture war is idolatry. It is a war of worship. Until people bow the knee and confess Jesus Christ as Lord, the culture war cycle will continue. But there is much the church can do to aid in God's work. The gospel of Jesus Christ must become our center. We need a clear position that does not instill shame but offers God's loving grace and revealed will, not just for our sexuality but for our whole lives.

Jesus bought my body on the cross, and my body is not mine to do with it what I will. My ethical stance on gay sex doesn't define me, nor does it disqualify me from being part of the gay *or* Christian community. Even if you disagree with my conclusions—what I sincerely hold out as hard fought truth to you—the fact remains that God loves you and desires relationship with you. It's only in this love that we know who we are, and have true moral knowledge.

I was simply someone who encountered the love of God in Jesus Christ and had my life turned upside down. I am no longer my own. My identity as a gay man is a temporary reality that will soon be transformed. It could never be greater than Jesus' claim on my life.

Are we willing to give up our identities, and the power associated with them, for the sake of knowing Christ? Are we willing to admit our errors? Are we willing to step, like Jesus, across cultural lines and offer his grace and forgiveness? Are we willing to love and listen to our enemies? I long to see the day we are.

Will you join me? I invite you to come into the Father's loving arms, where our most desperate battles are won and where you, through following Christ, will become forever the person you were created to be.

This is the battle of a lifetime. This is the longing we were made for: always satisfied, never satiated. This is the Christian way—utterly human yet full of God's Spirit.

This is the war of loves.

And day by day, tear by tear, heart by heart, it is being won.

APPENDIX I

WHAT I LEARNED THE SCRIPTURES REALLY SAY ABOUT HOMOSEXUALITY

Biblical commands are not arbitrary decrees but correspond to the way the world is and will be.

—*Richard Bauckham*

Did God really say . . .

—*Genesis 3:1*

So what did I discover the Bible really says about homosexuality? What I write here comes from an ever-evolving understanding. It has developed over a decade of existential wrestling with God, as well as through study at Oxford and elsewhere. Ultimately, I found that when I surrendered my sexual desires to the lordship of Jesus, the biblical texts became much clearer and sharper.

What follows is my understanding at this point in my journey and in my scholarly development. (Some of the terminology in this section will require patience.) Whether you agree or disagree with my conclusions, I recommend you keep searching with God, while prioritizing the importance of Jesus Christ through the Scriptures, reason, and Christian tradition. I would encourage you to refer to the list of resources at the end of this book, where I outline a few scholars I recommend for further reading.

GENESIS AND JESUS

As I started to read Jesus' words in the Gospels, I saw that marriage was, in and of itself, between a man and a woman. In Matthew 19:4–5, Jesus quotes directly from the creation narrative in Genesis 1–3: "'Haven't you read,' he replied, 'that at the beginning the Creator "made them male and female," and said, "For this reason a man will leave his father and mother and be united to his wife, and the two will become one flesh"?'" Jesus says that he is relaunching God's original project of creation, which was interrupted by broken worship and sin.

It was necessary for Jesus to emphasize the word of the Creator in addition to the mere act of creating, or the result of it. He reminds his hearers of the significance of sexual difference, and the significance of marriage between one man and woman, which had ceased to be morally apparent when it came to the contentious problem of divorce. Jesus is clarifying that for a male and a female to become husband and wife—by leaving their families behind and becoming sexually one, forming a new kinship unit—that is not just "how things normally go" but how God has made them and *wishes* them to be understood:

what scholar Bernd Wannenwetsch has called "the norm as ought."[39]

If Jesus, the supreme interpreter of the Old Testament, God in the flesh, reaffirmed this teaching, how could I keep resisting it and call him Lord? Also, Jesus, as the one who fulfilled the law of Moses, says that not one "tittle" will pass from it, including such keenly relevant passages as Leviticus 18 and 20, which clearly condemn same-sex practice. In this sense, when Jesus, as a Jewish rabbi, forbids sexual immorality *(porneai)* in Mark 7:21, it would refer to, at bare minimum, the Old Testament law and thus same-sex practice. Jesus saw himself as fulfilling a specific way of living, anchored in the requirements of and relationship with Israel's God, his Father, developed over hundreds of years. This was not just a culturally relative definition of immorality.

BACK TO THE BIBLE?

Obviously, there are no quick and easy answers to how we relate to all the Old Testament laws. But does that mean we can pick and choose from them at our leisure? No.

As I reflected further, the old argument comparing shellfish and mixed fibers with same-sex activity in Leviticus 18 and 20 no longer held up when I put the whole story of Scripture together. The legal injunctions of Leviticus and other Old Testament books were written to set Israel apart from the nations that surrounded them, as a sign and outreach to them but also to morally instruct God's people. There is no neat divide between ritual purity and moral purity in the Old Covenant, as they were equated in a way they are no longer in the New Covenant. In the early church, the division between Gentile and Jew was undone by Jesus' life, death and resurrection, making "one new humanity out of the two" (Eph. 2:14–15).

This provided a new means of fulfilling the covenant and putting those outside of Israel's relationship with God in right relationship with him by grace through Christ's faithfulness. It also fulfilled and did away with the temple and its system of sacrifice. Those purity laws relating to shellfish and fibers listed in Leviticus had been fulfilled in the Messiah, but the moral injunctions still provided the basis of moral instruction for the early church and Christians today.

Those who belonged to God were no longer marked by things like not eating shrimp. Rather they were marked by obedience and faith in Israel's Messiah, empowered by the Holy Spirit. Particularly in this case, their personal faith was expressed by abstaining from sexual immorality and living in purity provided by the Holy Spirit.

In Acts 15, the early church met to rule on Paul's view that the Jewish purity laws were no longer applicable to Gentile believers, nor were they the source of God's righteous action in reckoning Gentile Christ followers righteous. Just before outlawing sexual immorality, Peter affirms all whom God adopts: "God, who knows the heart, showed that he accepted [Gentiles] by giving the Holy Spirit to them, just as he did to us. He did not discriminate between us and them, for he purified their hearts by faith (Acts 15:8–9).

God does not discriminate, but he calls believers of all kinds to a standard. While Jesus' death and resurrection is the only source of right standing with God, the early church ruled that all sexual immorality was still forbidden.

PAUL'S LETTERS

As I became more and more comfortable with my decision to be celibate, I could face the Scriptures that I previously found the most confronting. I came to see in my studies at Oxford that the consensus of the vast majority of Pauline scholars, from both the more critical and the more orthodox sides, confirmed that same-sex practice was understood by Paul implicitly as a normal part of fallen humanity. I respected those who admitted that Paul thought same-sex activity was wrong, even if in a loving, committed relationship, but just disagreed with him.

Same-sex desire, like other desires that find their root in the fall, is part of the reality of the broken creation. God is right to save Gentiles through Christ and not through legal obedience to Old Testament law, which had to do with maintenance of an older covenant. We are all broken worshipers, regardless of our orientation or identity. None of us have the right to judge, but this does not change the righteous standard we all fall short of. Jesus alone met that standard for us, and by the power of the Holy Spirit, we can live into it.

N. T. Wright states, "There are no surprises on this in the Bible. For Jews, homosexual behavior wasn't an issue [because it was assumedly out of bounds], except as part of a larger whole to which Jesus refers in traditional biblical terms. For non-Jews, such as those addressed by Paul, it was an obvious issue, since every possible kind of sexual expression was well known in cities like Corinth and Rome (there is a popular belief just now that the ancients didn't know about lifelong same-sex relationships, but this is easily refuted by the evidence both literary and archaeological)."[40]

While there was a general understanding of homosexual acts in the broader Greco-Roman literature of the time as predominantly virile or exploitative expressions of power over another, many counterexamples of loving gay romances and gay love poetry that would echo and resemble a gay marriage also existed, including the Greek tradition of writing on homoerotic love.[41]

There were gay love affairs during the time of emperors such as Caesar Augustus and throughout Greco-Roman history. The emperor Hadrian fell in love with Antinous, who then was made a god in Rome's worship.

While I once believed that Paul never would have heard of an erotic, gay relationship or "marriage" of mutual affectation, I came to realize in my studies that this was historically inaccurate and clutching at straws. In verses 25–26 of the first chapter of Romans, Paul uses the terms *kata physin* ("according to nature") and *para physin* ("against nature"). These terms refer to a definition of human nature that isn't determined by innate desires or an internalist view of nature (like philosopher Friedrich Nietzsche describes) or power and identity politics (like Michel Foucault or Judith Butler describe). Rather our behavior either does or doesn't align with our *original* role to give proper worship to God according to the image in which he made us.

Wesley Hill notes, "Male and female is the creational intention not because we can see that clearly in our present contexts but rather because it is given to us in the pre-fall, pre-sin-and-death narratives of Genesis 1 and 2."[42]

In Judaism, human nature was related to our role as priests and worshipers in God's creation, his "temple" or sacred space. We are like God's mini living statues, which in ancient Near Eastern culture would represent a particular god in its temple.

Unlike these false gods, however, Yahweh Elohim's image and likeness was etched on living, breathing human beings. In the Greco-Roman world, "proper use" sums up an approach to human nature. In this context, Paul writes that same-sex acts are counter to the image of God, meaning they do not fit his intentions for worship of him in the sacred space of the world.

In Romans 1, Paul's famous text on homosexuality, same-sex sexual expression is symbolic of all human sin because it represents an inversion of the physical reality of being made male-female in the image of God. Paul is not describing gay people but the effect of sin's entry into the world that has meant we all have desire that runs counter to God's purposes and image.

Human nature was the same then as it is today, and Paul was certainly aware of same-sex-attracted people like me. There are a myriad of other complex and broken desires that are reflected in his vice lists, but he chose same-sex practice in Romans 1 in order to portray sin as a twisting or inversion of God's purposes for our bodies and lives. Remarkably, he doesn't start just with the Levitical reference to two men but includes two women in the picture. This reflects the greater notion in rabbinic thinking of the time that all same-sex practice was wrong. Yet for Paul, as this passage describes, these desires could never disqualify one from receiving the love of God, and in repentance, entering the kingdom of God. They have the power to do so only if one makes them one's ultimate identity, rejecting God's salvation in Christ. Think about that! This was *revolutionary*.

In the first verse of Romans 2, Paul writes, "You, therefore, have no excuse, you who pass judgment on someone else, for at whatever point you judge another, you are condemning yourself, because you who pass judgment do the same things."

Paul here comments that sin is a universal issue. Not only do the Jews do the same things as the Gentiles, but the root problem is the same—putting something created into the position of the Creator. Paul then outlines in Romans 3:23 that all of us fall short of the glory of God. Paul is clear that same-sex acts (as with the other vices listed) are a universal reality across cultures and time, reaching into our own.

New Testament scholar Richard B. Hays states, "In sharp contrast to the immediate recollections of the creation story, Paul portrays homosexual behavior as a 'sacrament' of the anti-religion of human beings who refuse to honor God."[43] Augustine's solution is summed up in his axiom "Love God and do as you please,"[44] and in this passage, Paul shows that in our self-death to these desires for God, we find a transformative, new, and holy pleasure: true worship of God in the Messiah.

Another passage that made new sense to me was 1 Corinthians 6:9. There Paul transliterates the Hebrew terms *mishav* ["one who lies with"—*koites,* in ancient Greek] and *zakur* [male—*arsen,* in ancient Greek] from the Greek translation of the Jewish Old Testament (LXX) in Leviticus 18 and 20.[45] He then forms a brand-new term in 1 Corinthians 6 by fusing *arseno* with *koites* to describe homosexual practice. This new construction, *arseno-koites,* is a general term used to translate the Jewish sexual ethic in Leviticus 18 and 20 to the Gentile world, even though other, often more negative and specific Greek terms already existed for homosexual people. Paul insists in 1 Corinthians 6:11 that some of the believers in the Corinthian church, as would have been the case in any population of people, used to be *arsenokoites,* or people who sleep with members of the same sex: "That is what some of you were. But you were washed, you were sanctified, you were justified in the name of the Lord Jesus Christ and by the Spirit of our God."

E. P. Sanders, one of the most prominent Pauline scholars and himself liberal on the question of homosexuality, agrees that "Paul himself condemned homosexual activity and warned his converts against the pleasures of the flesh, but he did not prohibit passion and desire within marriage."[46] Anytime such a vice list is mentioned, the inference is that there are many in the community who have been redeemed out of behaviors that made these desires ultimate identities.

Why does all this matter? Because far from having my heart crushed, I felt seen by the Bible. Rather than condemning me, these passages indicated my full acceptance, like these earliest Christians, in the church as a gay man with these desires and affirmed my choice to no longer live according to them. The gospel of Jesus Christ, as preached by Paul, is not a law-free gospel but a gospel that reoriented Jewish practices around the Messiah who had come, and that required non-Jewish people to abstain from sexual immorality, including same-sex practice. It was oddly satisfying, oddly *normalizing,* to see my struggle not as the exotic twistedness of some generation far removed from the early church but as a perennial struggle. Around me, I suddenly felt, was a great company of witnesses—yes, gay believers from every age who had to reckon with these desires, these questions. And some of them, undoubtedly, found the answers. I was *so* not alone.

N. T. Wright states, "People often suggest that since Paul believed in grace, not law, all the old rules were swept away in a new era of 'tolerance,' but this is a shallow and trivial view. Paul (and most early Christians known to us, right through the centuries) stuck with the bare essentials of Jewish morality: no worship of idols, no sex outside marriage."[47]

Today, God's radical inclusion is offered to all in Christ, but that full acceptance does not deny the moral guidance of the Scriptures. These same laws in Scripture were upheld by the early church, even if they recognized that the law was unable to provide the ultimate salvation found in the Messiah Jesus.

Reading these passages is very hard for anyone who is gay or same-sex attracted, but Wesley Hill reminds us, "One of the most striking things about the New Testament teaching on homosexuality is that, right on the heels of the passages that condemn homosexual activity, there are, without exception, resounding affirmations of God's extravagant mercy and redemption. God condemns homosexual behavior and amazingly, profligately, at great cost to himself, lavishes his love on homosexual persons."[48]

God did this in my life, and these passages—yes, *these very passages that once made me feel the weight of condemnation*—have now become reminders of God's love and grace. In Romans 8:38–39, Paul reminds us that "neither death nor life, neither angels nor demons, neither the present nor the future, nor any powers, neither height nor depth, nor anything else in all creation, will be able to separate us from the love of God that is in Christ Jesus our Lord."

Certainly, that includes homosexuality. And in that boundless, never-separating love, I was able to find what God wanted to say to me by his Word all along.

APPENDIX 2

DESIRING AND IMAGING GOD: THE CHALLENGES

MARRIAGE NOW AND THEN

A significant moment in my journey was when I realized that God did not create humans as male and female as a statement to oppress LGBTQI people or because God is a homophobic projection of our culture (although, without our idols removed, God can and has easily become so). Rather, as the author of Genesis writes and then Jesus reiterates, God created us as male and female so we would *reflect his image together.*

The diversity of male and female are vital for God-given relational diversity in the church. This diversity of male and female is God's means to fill the earth with his own image and likeness, as well as to restore the sacred garden of Eden in his new creation.

The Creator wanted to share his own loving nature not with a humanity that was boringly uniform but with a human family that was colorfully diverse, in body and redeemed personhood. Christopher West states, "Each person of the Trinity is unique, unrepeatable, and distinct from the others. Yet each is himself in virtue of his relation to the others, that is, in virtue of the eternal mystery of self-giving and community at the heart of the Trinitarian Life."[49] Each marriage between a man and a woman is a microcosm of God's vision for unity in diversity. This human unity-in-diversity has been broken by the fall, yet Jesus Christ, the heavenly man, restored this image in his life, death, and resurrection.

The author of Genesis iterates, "Then God said, 'Let us make man *in our image, after our likeness.* And let them have dominion over the fish of the sea and over the birds of the heavens and over the livestock and over all the earth and over every creeping thing that creeps on the earth.' So God created man *in his own image, in the image of God* he created him; male and female he created them" (1:26–27 ESV, emphasis added). Out of this union came procreative life, just as out of the unity of the godhead, God created the whole cosmos. Marriage was envisaged by God as a sacred kinship between male and female—a one-flesh union reflecting the God who is love.

In Genesis 2:18 ("It is not good for the man to be alone. I will make a helper suitable for him") and 2:20 ("For Adam no suitable helper was found"), the word translated as "suitable" is *kenegdo,* which is used to describe Eve as being "opposite/alike" Adam.[50] These human persons are distinct in bodily sex yet alike. They are equally human.

This distinction inscribed in the bodies of Eve and Adam matters because God's plan of salvation, revealed in the marriage of Christ and his church, is yet to come. The other aspect of biblical marriage that reflects God's intention is the word used of Eve, *ezer,* which means "helper" or "reinforcement in battle."[51] By himself, Adam is weak and exposed, and the same is true for

Eve without him. Eve is a coequal and a person distinct from Adam, made to partner with him in their call to love God and care for his creation.

The implication is that Adam needs Eve, and Eve needs Adam, in order to image God. They cannot socially or biologically work without each other. They are incomplete without God and without each other. They need each other's diversity. Together they both make up the original humanity. Without each other, they are lost, incomplete, and unable to fulfill God's commands.

Sam Allberry says, "If marriage [between a man and woman] shows us the shape of the Gospel, then celibacy shows us the sufficiency of it."[52] Marriage is at the heart of the kingdom that Jesus came to bring into this world.

CELIBACY NOW AND THEN

Of course, marriage between a man and a woman is not the only relational situation that reflects God's image and likeness. It is, however, the only one that involves sexual intercourse, or coming together as "one flesh." This is vital, as often in the conversation, we argue about sexual ethics or falsely equate sex and intimacy, and neglect God's broader invitation to create alternative family structures that fulfill our human need for intimacy.

The church itself became an alternative family structure that didn't fit societal norms, by embracing the minorities the ancient world looked down on, including slaves, women, and sexual minorities like the eunuch from Ethiopia. For its entire history, the church has always created and fostered diverse community structures, whether monasteries, missional communities, or small cells of believers like the Celtic priories. They are an essential of church community, not just add-ons to "family" churches.

In Scripture, we see how God worked through friendships like David and Jonathan, Naomi and Ruth, Jesus and John, Paul and Timothy. God used the love in these various friendships to express truths about his coming kingdom; for example, God's adoption of the Gentiles was foreshadowed in Ruth's story and her covenant faithfulness to Naomi.

In 1 Samuel 18:1, we see the unique spirit-to-spirit love of David and Jonathan. This is not a homoerotic or "one-flesh union" like a marriage but a self-sacrificial friendship: "After David had finished talking with Saul, Jonathan became one in spirit with David, and he loved him as himself." They shared a love that was "wonderful, more wonderful than that of women" (2 Sam. 1:26). Jonathan helped David escape from Saul, then later died alongside his father and brothers. David honored Jonathan after his death by adopting Jonathan's lame relative into his court.

Similarly, John was the only disciple of the Twelve who was at the cross when Jesus was abandoned by his other followers and friends. This is witnessed in John 19:26: "When Jesus saw his mother and the disciple whom he loved standing nearby, he said to his mother, 'Woman, behold, your son!'" (ESV). We see Jesus forming this first kingdom nonnuclear family through the spiritual bond he shared with John and Mary. The church is a family bound not by physical lineage but by the spiritual bond of knowing Jesus.

When we look at the covenant friendship of David and Jonathan, and of Jesus and John, we see that marriage is not ultimate or even the greatest form of intimacy that can be experienced, as is often wrongly communicated by the church and our society at large. Rather the love of friendship is the greatest of the loves.

There is a long and rich Christian tradition that has prized this. Of course, marriage is profound and contains friendship itself, but the point here is that a life of celibacy as a gay man does not, as I thought originally, cut me off from the intimacy I was made for.

The lie I had believed was that I must have gay sex to be whole. Like many gay people, my outrage at the church for denying gay marriage came from the belief that sex is a requirement for human flourishing. I came to realize that gay marriage, for a Christian, is an oxymoron, as marriage is framed by God in the Scriptures as solely between a man and a woman. Claiming it can be anything else is to argue from scriptural silence. The practical reality is that friendship not only suffices for me but is the greatest love there is to experience. I don't need marriage.

THE PROPHETIC PARADOX OF CELIBACY

We often hear people say in the Christian church that celibacy was designed only as a gift for a select few. Nothing could be farther from the truth. Celibacy is a theme seen throughout Scripture. The eunuch has a greater progeny (name) than those who can have nuclear families. In Acts 8, the Ethiopian eunuch, we presume, although we're not told this in Scripture, becomes the first spiritual father of the continent of Africa.

Our culture worships erotic love, insisting sex is necessary for human flourishing or, as understood in many polytheistic societies, for "the blessing of the gods." When we in the church elevate marriage or romance above God, we fail to see the prophetic paradox of Jesus' own life.[53] Jesus broke this sexual idol by living as "[a eunuch] for the sake of the kingdom of heaven" (Matt. 19:12).

By adopting this marriageless existence, Jesus embodied a prophetic stance against the rejection of sexual minorities from the temple in Jerusalem, as well as in Greco-Roman society. Not only that, he lived a sexual life that was defined by the restored future, not the broken present. Side B Christians (and other singles) imitate Jesus in this way. We become eunuchs for the sake of the kingdom. We are not sexless, but rather the lack we may feel becomes the place for fullness and glory of God, and the growth of God's family.

Eunuchs or those who were sexually impotent were generally despised and exploited in the ancient royal courts of Greco-Roman culture.[54] Lucian of Samosata records the words of an opponent of a eunuch vying for a chair of philosophy in Athens, which reflect a common attitude toward sexual minorities in the ancient world: "The eunuch is neither man nor woman, but something composite, hybrid and monstrous, alien to human nature."[55] Interestingly, Michel Foucault describes a similar view of homosexuality in medical and religious discourse in the early to late modern era as "an hermaphroditism of the soul."[56] Such a view is plainly unscriptural and not reflective of God's heart. Jesus takes the suffering of LGBTQI people into his own life and suffers alongside them as their Messiah and Savior.

Part of Jesus' cross and his death and suffering was giving up the possibility of having children. This is one of the sufferings that people who are celibate carry with Jesus, identified in his going to the cross, unable to have children or a family. In such a way, celibate followers of Jesus become "eunuchs for the sake of the kingdom of heaven" (Matt. 19:12). It is in this "becoming a eunuch" that God promises a name and progeny superior to even having children or an earthly legacy, as seen in Isaiah 56:4–5 (ESV):

> Thus says the Lord:
> "To the eunuchs who keep my Sabbaths,
> who choose the things that please me
> and hold fast my covenant,
> I will give in my house and within my walls
> a monument and a name
> *better than sons and daughters;*
> I will give them an everlasting name
> that shall not be cut off."

When we are willing to be single, even for a time in our life, God promises to give us a name, a monument, and an everlasting progeny that will not be cut off. This progeny is the children of God in the church. The name is that of Jesus Christ. Becoming a eunuch for the sake of the kingdom of heaven is a sacred form of sacrificial love toward God. If that is the default calling for Christians like me, as it was for Christ, unless otherwise called to the rare option of a mixed-orientation marriage, then we can have nothing but overflowing joy.

IMAGING GOD: RESISTING THE COMMODIFICATION OF DESIRE

The world sees our value reflected in our romantic status. One result of this is that we are seeing unprecedented rates of suicide and loneliness.[57] This focus on our relational and sexual desires is only making us more miserable.

My story has taught me that as Christians, we have the privilege of showing the world what it looks like to no longer live under the constant oppression of desire, especially sexual desire. The Christian has forsaken this worldly commodification in order to be a bright signpost of God's love reflected in Christ, and a foretaste of his coming kingdom.

For me, the war of loves was won only after I died to my sexuality and intimacy was given back to me in the form of spiritual friendships. The church still has a long way to go in making a life like mine not just practicable but one of flourishing and joy, but God has worked despite the church's failures. He is faithful even when we are faithless.

Celibacy (or self-sacrifice in relationships), much like fasting or prayer, draws us more closely to the reality of the union we all experience as part of the church of Christ. Paul describes this union when he says, "Whoever is united [literally, married] with the Lord is one with him in spirit" (1 Cor. 6:17). For this reason, I actually find myself excited about God's invitation to live celibately. Celibacy leaves greater room for commitment to spiritual friendships and for dedicating my life to having spiritual children, like Paul did.

In his essay "The Body's Grace," Rowan Williams, the previous Archbishop of Canterbury, opens up the possibility for the commitment of two members of the same sex to embody God's triune love as a way of resisting this perversion of desire.[58] However, Williams does not face the difficult question of sexual difference in God's creation nor in the sacred analogy of Christ, the Bridegroom, and the church, his bride.

I contend that when God says in Leviticus 18:22, "Do not have sexual relations with a man as one does with a woman; that is detestable," he does so for a reason related to his image, not just for the sake of ritual purity. In the life of Israel, God's image was to be reflected in his people. Any behavior that departed from his law was idolatry and was contrary to their image-bearing nature. The same is true for us. Anything not done in faith in God falls short of true worship. This is the meaning of sin, and it leads to death or spiritual disconnection.

Paul teaches that exchanging the image of God for another image in anything we do (as expressed in male-male and female-female pairing, as Paul outlined in Romans 1) represents a rejection of God himself. As the Center for Faith, Sexuality, and Gender states, "The Fall has corrupted God's original intent for human sexuality in all persons; therefore, all people—straight or non-straight—experience corruption in their sexuality."[59] Any departure from God's intention for sexual expression in marriage misses the mark.

For these reasons and others, I remain unconvinced by arguments affirming same-sex marriage. They rest on the presupposition that same-sex desire wasn't ever understood by biblical authors as involving faithful monogamy in the ancient Near Eastern and Greco-Roman period. If we didn't worship romantic love as a god, I honestly believe, the culture war over sexuality would cease. In Christ, a new creation has dawned, and one day, same-sex and broken heterosexual desire will be no longer, but until then we groan inwardly for our resurrection and the fulfillment of God's coming kingdom.

That said, gay unions and relationships, as many of mine did, can contain deep commitment, friendship, and sacrificial love that, when separated from sexual expression, I am sure, are important to God and are to be honored in these ways as forms of friendship. The church has often, although not always, failed by either celebrating and affirming these relationships and thus changing church doctrine or rejecting them altogether. Neither approach is helpful. There is nuance in each situation.

The God-honoring parts of gay relationships can be enjoyed within God's vision for friendship. Human beings can live without sex, but we cannot live without love. God calls us to repent of sinful sexual relationships. I have many friends who have left gay marriages or relationships to follow Jesus.

The redemption of LGBTQI Christians takes a unique form that the church must learn from, and learn to embrace and empower. The church must also learn how to invite gay couples into it without working against the grace God is pouring out in their lives as he calls them to holiness. This requires relinquishing condescension and embracing humility and patience. As my story demonstrates, it took years to receive what I needed from God before I was willing to live differently and leave gay relationships behind.

My view is that when a gay person becomes a Christian, they must not repress or indulge their erotic longings or base their entire identity on such desires. Rather they need to remember that these longings originate from a more fundamental desire for God himself. The only way same-sex desire can be safely understood is first when it is, as Sarah Coakley says, "both understood in relation to and in its uniqueness from others of its kind, rooted first in a desire for God and therefore, capable of purification or elevation."[60]

Same-sex erotic desires are part of our fallen humanity. They are similar to broken heterosexual desires in that their end can never be righteously expressed in the covenant of marriage. All human desire can be traced back to our desire for God, even if twisted by sin. I listen to my same-sex desires as part of my more fundamental craving for intimacy with God and others, and I also deny them in deference to desiring God's image, will, and person.

Denying same-sex desires simply to obey a law or to belong to the church not only fails but also is a miserable existence leading to sin. However, by understanding that my desires actually point to my desire for God in Christ and in the Holy Spirit, I have come to a place of satisfaction and joy in my celibacy.

Just like bad marriages, there can be bad celibacy. I always recommend that anyone struggling with their desires, but especially all new Christ followers, give God a year to reveal the real root of those desires and to give them answers to the relational challenges they face. Like Christ, who went to the cross, all people must die to themselves in order to live in the new way of resurrection.

Our sinful desires emerge from what Scripture calls the "flesh" or "old man." We give them over to purification where new, holy desires, ecstatic and from the new creation reality, are able to arise. They are part of the new person one becomes in Christ. In doing so, we don't cease to be erotic or sexual without having sex; rather we redirect that energy into service and love for God and our neighbor. Those of us who are celibate start our heavenly vocation now, anticipating the future, in which there will be no marriage.

Because Christ has called me to celibacy, I have great joy. However, my lamentation is that celibate gay Christians like me are often rejected, dismissed, or at times ridiculed by other believers, for several reasons: because of our choice to surrender our sexuality to the lordship of Christ, because of our refusal to apologize for any aspect of gospel living, including sexual purity, and because of our loving acceptance of LGBTQI people. Sometimes we even become a liability in that if people encourage us or associate with us, they pay a social or political price. We live under a pressure few realize, which profoundly tests our trust in the Father.

The way ahead is difficult, as the church continues to deal with pressure, both from within and from outside, to compromise God's revealed truth. Simply changing the doctrine of the church is the most unloving thing that can be done for side B Christians like me. It makes an already tough path even harder. Sometimes it seems as if the idol of self and personal desires reigns everywhere, and there is little respite for Christians, especially celibate gay Christians. And yet God is at work, strengthening and transforming us and freeing us from the sin that attempt to enslave us. Our hope is in him.

I long for a future in which the church offers a clearer, more direct path to God for those who struggle with desire, especially for those in the beloved LGBTQI community. Jesus himself shows the way. His divine love leads us to abundant life and teaches us that any sacrifice for his sake can be transformed into richest ecstasy and joy. As celibate gay Christians, may we follow our beloved Savior, modeling his beautiful, holy vision for our bodies, desires, sexuality—our whole selves.

NOTES

1. C. S. Lewis, *Shadowlands* (London: William Nicholson, 1993).
2. Simon LeVay, "A Difference in Hypothalamic Structure between Heterosexual and Homosexual Men," *Science* 253 (1991): 1034–37. For further reading, see Simon LeVay, *Gay, Straight, and the Reason Why: The Science of Sexual Orientation*, 2nd ed. (New York: Oxford Univ. Press, 2016).
3. P. Lindström, "Brain Response to Putative Pheromones in Homosexual Men," *PNAS* 20 (2005): 7356–61. See a follow-up study published later on lesbians' pheromonal attraction.
4. J. Michael Bailey, Michael P. Dunne, and Nicholas G. Martin, "Genetic and Environmental Influences on Sexual Orientation and Its Correlates in an Australian Twin Sample," *Journal of Personality and Social Psychology* 78, no. 3 (2000): 524–36.
5. I. Savic, H. Berglund, and G. Dörner, "Neuroendocrine Response to Estrogen and Brain Differentiation in Heterosexuals, Homosexuals, and Transsexuals," *Archives of Sexual Behavior* 17, no. 1 (1988): 57–75.
6. Jean-Paul Sartre, *Existentialism and Humanism*, trans. (from French) Philip Mairet (London: Eyre Meuthuen, 1973), 65.
7. Aengus Carroll and Lucas Ramon Mendos, *State-Sponsored Homophobia: A World Survey of Sexual Orientation Laws: Criminalisation, Protection and Recognition*, 12th ed. (Geneva: ILGA, May 2017).

8. Richard Dawkins, *River out of Eden: A Darwinian View of Life* (New York: Basic Books, 1995), 17.
9. C. S. Lewis, *Mere Christianity* (London: Harper Collins, 2009), 29.
10. Michel Foucault, *Power/Knowledge: Selected Interviews and Other Writings, 1972–1977,* ed. Colin Gordon (New York: Pantheon, 1980), 73–74.
11. "You who are trying to be justified by law have been alienated from Christ; you have fallen away from grace" (Gal. 5:4).
12. See John Wesley's journey from the nominal Christian faith of his youth and early adulthood to the living faith of his adult years. The faith he received upon reading Paul's letter to the Romans spurred him on to seek—from his experiences of the Moravian Christians, who had absolute peace in suffering—what he called the "new faith." I was renewed in my understanding of how justification by faith applied to all aspects of my life, and particularly homosexuality. Like Wesley, I was liberated from the chains of a law-bound, self-justifying obedience. This is a danger today's evangelical churches must resist through the clear preaching of the gospel. Christian discipleship is an obedience through relational trust of a Person, knowing the free gift of God's self to us in Christ.
13. While I now call myself a celibate gay Christian, I mean this primarily in the descriptive sense. *Celibate* and *gay* are modifiers to the central noun, which is *Christian*. My ultimate identity is in Christ, related to the coming heavenly reality, where there will be perfect desire, perfect community, perfect love with perfect bodies before a perfect God. Celibacy becomes, then, a sign of this heaven as we wait for a day when Christ will fill and perfect everything, all in all.
14. To read my further thoughts on what I found the Bible really teaches on homosexuality and marriage, see appendix 1.
15. "A Sermon on the Estate of Marriage (1519)," trans. James Atkinson, in *Luther's Works,* ed. Helmut T. Lehmann, vol. 44, ed. James Atkinson (Philadelphia, 1966), 10.
16. Rudolf Brazda, *L'itineraire d'un triangle rose: La biographie d'un déporté pour motif d'homosexualité,* trans. Jean-Luc Schwab (2010).

17. Phil Davidson, "Rudolf Brazda: Last Known Survivor of the 'Pink Triangle' Gay Inmates of Nazi Concentration Camps," *Independent* (August 9, 2011), *www.independent.co.uk/news/obituaries/rudolf-brazda-last-known-survivor-of-the-pink-triangle-gay-inmates-of-nazi-concentration-camps-2334053.html.*
18. Ibid.
19. Ibid.
20. Søren Kierkegaard, *Provocations: Spiritual Writings of Kierkegaard,* ed. Charles Moore (New York: Plough, 2014), 193.
21. Wesley Hill, *Washed and Waiting: Reflections on Christian Faithfulness and Homosexuality* (Grand Rapids: Zondervan, 2010), 111.
22. See *The Four Loves* by C. S. Lewis.
23. Andrew Sullivan, *Love Undetectable: Notes on Friendship, Sex, and Survival* (New York: Random House, 1999), 198.
24. Matthew Vines, *God and the Gay Christian* (New York: Random House, 2014).
25. Henri Nouwen, *Lifesigns: Intimacy, Fecundity, and Ecstasy in Christian Perspective* (New York: Random House, 1989), 44.
26. See the exegesis of *'ezer* and *kenegdo* in Brian N. Peterson, "Does Genesis 2 Support Same-Sex Marriage? An Evangelical Response," *JETS* 60, no. 4 (2017): 681–96.
27. For example, the Reformation Project, Church Clarity.
28. See the different views surrounding the role of the law in John Perry's "Gentiles and Homosexuals: A Brief History of Analogy," especially Ben Witherington's and Richard Bauckham's interpretations.
29. Henri Nouwen, *The Life of the Beloved: Spiritual Living in a Secular World* (New York: Cross Road Publishing, 1992), 33.
30. Sarah Coakley, *The New Asceticism: Sexuality, Gender and the Quest for God* (London: Bloomsbury, 2015), 25.
31. There is a wide history of these kinds of gay cure therapies, but see Robert Colvile, "The Man Who Fried Gay People's Brains," *Independent* (July 6, 2016), *www.independent.co.uk/life-style/health-and-families/health-news/the-man-who-fried-gay-people-s-brains-a7119181.html.*
32. Augustine, *On Christian Doctrine (de doctrina Christiana),* book 1, trans. R. P. H. Green (Oxford: Oxford Univ. Press, 1997), I.1–5.

33. J. I. Packer, "Why I Walked: Sometimes Loving a Denomination Requires You to Fight," *Christianity Today* (January 1, 2003), *www.christianitytoday.com/ct/2003/january/6.46.html.*
34. A. Thiselton, "Realized Eschatology at Corinth," *New Testament Studies* 24, no. 4 (1978): 510–26, doi:10.1017/S0028688 50001451X.
35. Welsey Hill, "Once More: On the Label 'Gay Christian,'" *First Things* (February 1, 2013), *www.firstthings.com/blogs/firstthoughts/2013/02/once-more-on-the-label-gay-christian.*
36. David Foster Wallace, *This Is Water: Some Thoughts, Delivered on a Significant Occasion, about Living a Compassionate Life* (New York: Hachette, 2009), 10.
37. See Oliver O'Donovan's reflections in the Pilling Report (2013), compiled by the Church of England.
38. Dietrich Bonhoeffer, *Discipleship* (trans. 1948; London: SCM Press, 2006), 4.
39. Bernd Wannenwetsch, "Creation and Ethics: On the Legitimacy and Limitation of Appeals to 'Nature' in Christian Moral Reasoning," in Anthony Clarke and Andrew Moore, eds., *Within the Love of God: Essays on the Doctrine of God in Honour of Paul S. Fiddes* (Oxford: Oxford Univ. Press, 2014), *www.oxfordscholarship.com.*
40. N. T. Wright in Andrew Wilson, "Tom Wright on Homosexuality," *Think* (July 14, 2014), *http://thinktheology.co.uk/blog/article/tom_wright_on_homosexuality.*
41. E. P. Sanders, *Paul: The Apostle's Life, Letters and Thought* (London: SCM Press, 2016), 727–48.
42. Wesley Hill in Preston Sprinkle and Stanley N. Gundry, eds., *Two Views on Homosexuality, the Bible, and the Church* (Grand Rapids: Zondervan, 2016), 110.
43. Richard B. Hays, *The Moral Vision of the New Testament: A Contemporary Introduction to New Testament Ethics* (London: T&T Clark International, 1997), 386.
44. Found in the tract *In epistulam Ioannis ad Parthos* (Tractatus VII, 8), the passage reads, "Once for all, then, a short precept is given unto you: Love God, and do what you will: whether you hold your peace, through love hold your peace; whether you cry out,

through love cry out; whether you correct, through love correct; whether you spare, through love do you spare: In all things, let the root of love be within, for of this root can nothing spring but what is good."

45. Richard B. Hays, *The Moral Vision of the New Testament: A Contemporary Introduction to New Testament Ethics* (London: T&T Clark, 1997), 379–89.
46. E. P. Sanders, *Paul: The Apostle's Life, Letters, and Thought* (London: SCM Press, 2016), 747.
47. Wright in Wilson, "Tom Wright on Homosexuality."
48. Hill, *Washed and Waiting*, 62.
49. Christopher West, *Theology of the Body Explained: A Commentary on John Paul II's "Gospel of the Body"* (Leominster, UK: Gracewing, 2003), 119.
50. See commentary on *ezer* (helper) and *kenegdo* (opposite/alike) in Brian N. Peterson, "Does Genesis 2 Support Same-Sex Marriage? An Evangelical Response," *JETS* 60, no. 4 (2017): 681–96.
51. Ibid.
52. Sam Allberry, "How Celibacy Can Fulfill Your Sexuality," *Gospel Coalition* (August 26, 2016), *www.thegospelcoalition.org/article/how-celibacy-can-fulfill-your-sexuality/.*
53. Barry Danylak, *Redeeming Singleness: How the Storyline of Scripture Affirms the Single Life* (Wheaton, IL: Crossway, 2010), 83–115, 143–73.
54. Ibid., 154.
55. Ibid., 155.
56. Michel Foucault, *The History of Sexuality,* vol. 1: *An Introduction,* trans. Robert Hurley (New York: Random House, 1984), 43.
57. See the Samaritans' report on suicide and mental health: *www.samaritans.org/about-us/our-research/facts-and-figures-about-suicide.*
58. Rowan Williams, "The Body's Grace," *ABC* (August 24, 2011), *www.abc.net.au/religion/articles/2011/08/24/3301238.htm.*
59. See the Center for Faith, Sexuality and Gender's "Statement of Marriage, Sexuality and Gender," *www.centerforfaith.com.*
60. Sarah Coakley in Wesley Hill, "Faith's Desire: A Review of *God, Sexuality, and the Self*" (June 2014), *www.firstthings.com/article/2014/06/faiths-desire.*

GLOSSARY

LGBTQI: Lesbian, gay, bisexual, transgender, queer, intersex

Side A: Disagrees with Christian tradition, affirming a gay identity and seeing sexual expression in gay marriage as faithful to a Christian ethic

Side B: Affirms the Christian tradition; sees sexual expression in gay marriage as wrong but incorporates a gay identity under the lordship of Christ through celibacy and other forms of chastity

Side Y: Like side B but does not identify with the term LGBTQI. Prefers not to identify as gay but is more likely to use the term same-sex attracted or is reluctant to see sexual orientation as a category of identity or personhood

Side X: Claims either to no longer experience same-sex attraction or to be ex-gay and to have been freed by the process of sanctification

Intersex: A set of medical conditions with congenital anomaly of the reproductive and sexual system

Transgender: Denoting or relating to a person whose sense of personal identity and gender does not correspond with their birth sex

Gender dysphoria: The condition of feeling that one's emotional and psychological identity as male or female are opposite one's biological sex

Cisgender: Denoting or relating to a person whose sense of personal identity and gender corresponds with their birth sex

Queer: Generally used as an adjective for the LGBTQI community but also can refer to queer theory or queer theology, which are fields of academic discourse. Queer is often used to infer that one does not want to be limited, labelled, or expected to have simply one kind of attraction but has at some point been attracted to the same-sex.

Heteronormative: Denoting or relating to a worldview that promotes heterosexuality as the normal and preferred sexual orientation

RECOMMENDED RESOURCES

Note: These resources are diverse and may differ at points, but held together, they provide a broad picture I endorse.

Allberry, Samuel. *Is God Anti-Gay?*

Coles, Greg. *Single, Gay, Christian: A Personal Journey of Faith and Sexual Identity.*

Collins, Nate. *All But Invisible: Exploring Identity Questions at the Intersection of Faith, Gender, and Sexuality.*

Danylak, Barry. *Redeeming Singleness: How the Storyline of Scripture Affirms the Single Life.*

Hill, Wesley. *Spiritual Friendship: Finding Love in the Church as a Celibate Gay Christian.*

———. *Washed and Waiting: Reflections on Christian Faithfulness and Homosexuality.*

Hirsch, Debra. *Redeeming Sex: Naked Conversations about Sexuality and Spirituality.*

Nouwen, Henri. *Life of the Beloved: Spiritual Living in a Secular World.*

———. *Lifesigns: Intimacy, Fecundity, and Ecstasy in Christian Perspective.*

———. *The Wounded Healer: Ministry in Contemporary Society.*

Paris, Jenell Williams. *The End of Sexual Identity: Why Sex Is Too Important to Define Who We Are.*

Shaw, Ed. *The Plausibility Problem: The Church and Same-Sex Attraction.*

———. *Same-Sex Attraction and the Church: The Surprising Plausibility of the Celibate Life.*

Sprinkle, Preston. *Living in a Gray World: A Christian Teen's Guide to Understanding Homosexuality.*

———. *People to Be Loved: Why Homosexuality Is Not Just an Issue.*

Tushnet, Eve. *Gay and Catholic: Accepting My Sexuality, Finding Community, Living My Faith.*

West, Christopher. *Fill These Hearts: God, Sex, and the Universal Longing.*

Wilson, Todd. *Mere Sexuality: Rediscovering the Christian Vision of Sexuality.*

Yarhouse, Mark. *Homosexuality and the Christian: A Guide for Parents, Pastors, and Friends.*

Digging Deeper: Biblical Interpretation and Theological Ethics

Brock, Brian, and Bernd Wannenwetsch. *The Malady of the Christian Body: A Theological Exposition of Paul's First Letter to the Corinthians.* Eugene, OR: Wipf and Stock, 2016.

Coakley, Sarah. *The New Asceticism: Sexuality, Gender and the Quest for God* (especially last chapter). London: Bloomsbury, 2015.

Gathercole, Simon. "Sin in God's Economy: Agencies in Romans 1 and 7," in *Divine and Human Agency in Paul and His Cultural Environment.* London: T&T Clark, 2008.

Goddard, Andrew. *God, Gentiles and Gay Christians.* Cambridge: Grove, 2001.

———. *Homosexuality and the Church of England.* Cambridge: Grove, 2004.

Grenz, Stanley J. *Welcoming but Not Affirming: An Evangelical Response to Homosexuality.* Louisville: Westminster/John Knox Press, 1998.

Hays, Richard B. "Homosexuality," in *The Moral Vision of the New Testament: A Contemporary Introduction to New Testament Ethics.* San Francisco: HarperSanFranciso, 1996.

Hooker, Morna D. "Adam in Romans 1," in *From Adam to Christ: Essays on Paul*. Cambridge: Cambridge Univ. Press, 2008.
O'Donovan, Oliver. *A Conversation Waiting to Begin: The Churches and the Gay Controversy*. London: SCM Press, 2009.
Roberts, Christopher C. *Creation and Covenant: The Significance of Sexual Difference in the Moral Theology of Marriage*. London: T&T Clark, 2007.
Saint Andrews Day Statement. *www.ceec.info/st-andrews-day-statement.html*.
Sanders, E. P. *Paul: The Apostle's Life, Letters, and Thought* (particularly appendix 1 on homosexuality in the Greco-Roman world and the chapter on 1 Corinthians 6). Minneapolis: Fortress Press, 2016.
Sprinkle, Preston and Stanley N. Gundry, eds. *Two Views on Homosexuality, the Bible, and the Church*. Grand Rapids: Zondervan, 2016.
Swartley, Willard. *Homosexuality: Biblical Interpretation and Moral Discernment*. Scottdale, PA: Herald Press, 2003.
Via, Dan O. and Robert A. J. Gagnon. *Homosexuality and the Bible: Two Views*. Minneapolis: Fortress Press, 2004.
West, Christopher. *Theology of the Body Explained: A Commentary on John Paul II's "Gospel of the Body"* Leominster, UK: Gracewing, 2003.

Recommended Websites

The Center for Faith, Sexuality and Gender. *www.centerforfaith.com*.
The Institute for the Study of Sexual Identity. *www.sexualidentityinstitute.org*.
Living Out. *www.livingout.org*.
Revoice. *www.revoice.us*.
Spiritual Friendship. *www.spiritualfriendship.org*.

Other Important or Differing Views

Brownson, James V. *Bible, Gender, Sexuality: Reframing the Church's Debate on Same-Sex Relationships*. Grand Rapids: Eerdmans, 2013.
DeFranza, Megan K. *Sex Difference in Christian Theology: Male, Female, and Intersex in the Image of God*. Grand Rapids: Eerdmans, 2015

Lee, Justin. *Torn: Rescuing the Gospel from the Gays-vs-Christians Debate.* New York: Jericho Books, 2012.
Perry, John. "The Author Replies . . . Vocation and Creation: Beyond the Gentile-Homosexual Analogy." *Journal of Religious Ethics* 40, no. 2 (2012): 385–400.
Perry, John. "Gentiles and Homosexuals: A Brief History of an Analogy." *Journal of Religious Ethics* 38, no. 2 (2010): 321–47.
Rae, Murray. *More Than a Single Issue: Theological Considerations Concerning the Ordination of Practising Homosexuals.* Hindmarsh: Australian Theological Forum, 2000.
Song, Robert. *Covenant and Calling: Towards a Theology of Same-Sex Relationships.* London: SCM Press, 2014.
Vines, Matthew. *God and the Gay Christian.* New York: Convergent, 2014.